MRS DARLEY'S PAGAN WHISPERS

*A Celebration of Pagan Festivals, Sacred Days,
Spirituality and Traditions of the Year*

MRS DARLEY'S PAGAN WHISPERS

*A Celebration of Pagan Festivals, Sacred Days,
Spirituality and Traditions of the Year*

Carole Carlton

First edition
Published in Great Britain
By Mirage Publishing 2008

A CIP catalogue record for this book
Is available from the British Library.

ISBN: 978-1-90257-835-4

Mirage Publishing
PO Box 161
Gateshead
NE8 4WW
Great Britain

Printed and bound in Great Britain by

Book Printing UK
Remus House, Coltsfoot Drive, Woodston, Peterborough, PE2 9JX

Cover © Mirage Publishing
Layout by Artistic Director Sharon Anderson

Papers used in the production of this book are recycled,
thus reducing environmental depletion.

To Willie, who has honoured my path
and allowed me to find myself.

Contents

Preface   9
Introduction   11

1. A Whisper of Yesterday   15
2. Spinning the Wheel   29
3. The Festival of Imbolc (Imbolg or Oimelc)   31
4. The Festival of the Spring Equinox   47
5. The Festival of Beltane   61
6. The Festival of the Summer Solstice   83
7. The Festival of Lughnasadh   99
8. The Festival of the Autumnal Equinox   115
9. The Festival of Samhain   129
10. The Winter Solstice   145
11. A Promise of Tomorrow   167

Other Titles   168

Preface

An Invitation to Travel the Spiritual Path

The light of the moon shone intermittently in the November sky, as I sank beside the roaring fire in Mrs Darley's cottage. 'Listen,' she whispered and pointed towards the window. 'Whenever the wind blows from the east and the wind chimes dance in the moonlight, there is magic in the air.'

Those words were magical to me then and still remain so, as they became my invitation to step into the void and begin to explore my own spirituality within the beauty of an ancient Cornish landscape.

I gradually came to understand that no matter how much we long for modern comforts or to shut out the cold and inclement weather, part of us yearns for a meaningful relationship with nature and, somewhere deep within each one of us, the rhythm of the earth's natural drum still beats. It was this rhythm that I was determined to unearth and make a part of my life, and it was at this point that I began the quest for my own holy grail.

The quest (which still goes on) has taken me far and wide, in many directions, and always brought me into contact with those who have already connected with their own deep well of knowing and, by following their example, I trust that I too will eventually drink from my own inner realms.

Upon moving to Cornwall in 1991, I became bewitched by its enchanting timeless beauty, which captured my heart and holds me still. Brooding and mysterious, the south-eastern edge of Bodmin Moor provided the wild backdrop against which the introduction to my magical training and love of nature began. It was here, through the often bizarre, yet strangely compelling, guidance of Mrs Darley, that I began to experience my own connection to the universe, and to the forces of nature. I became aware of the existence and polarity of a Divine female and male presence both within the landscape and within myself. Gradually my interest gained momentum through other teachers I met along the path and to whom I am also indebted.

This book is an eclectic mixture of history, myth and folklore, coupled with poetry and thought-provoking tales, which is my own personal way of acknowledging the sacred cycle of life, death and rebirth.

I would like to invite you to savour every moment of this experiential journey. Feel the energies of the earth, listen to them calling on the wind, whispering their secrets and beckoning you to explore their mysteries. Enjoy a year of ebbing and flowing, of magical discoveries, and allow yourself to encounter the Divine essence which lives in us all.

Introduction

Permission to Travel the Spiritual Path

'So what exactly are you?' I am often asked. 'A Pagan, a Pantheist, a follower of the Goddess or of the God?'

I am none of these things and yet, paradoxically, I am all of these things.

It is almost as if we are compelled by society to have a label, whether this is our name, our job title, our political persuasion, our sexuality or our religion. As a result we often seek our identity in groups, where there is safety in numbers, and hence we become afraid to step outside the tried and tested, for fear of retribution, alienation, or ridicule. This is never as true as with the choice of our spiritual path or chosen religious doctrine.

When we are born into this world, we are given a label in the form of a family name and become part of that specific group or family 'tribe'. Inevitably we begin to take on the tribe's beliefs, likes, dislikes, fears, habits, religious beliefs, political persuasions and a myriad of other subtle nuances, which give us a sense of 'belonging'. Initially, of course, this is both necessary and inevitable as we are totally dependant upon those older than ourselves to tend to our basic needs and to teach us certain things about the environment in which we live.

When we look back, however, not very much of what we were taught ourselves, or indeed what we teach our children, is objective. The majority of teachings are based on the personal opinions or belief structures of parents, teachers and significant others, which we hear or experience so often during our formative years that they become ingrained and are often almost impossible to shake loose. We become paralysed with fear and guilt, obsessed by 'labels' and become unable to question the reasoning behind our beliefs or indeed realise that it is acceptable to challenge them. Sometimes we simply need to give ourselves permission to break free from the confines of the tribe and find our own way.

There is a wonderful quotation taken from *The Second Messiah* by Knight and Lomas (1997):

'We all like to think of ourselves as open minded, but often we are the person who stands face inward, chanting "this is the only high ground, this is all there is"'.

We feel safe on familiar ground, the tried and tested, the accepted, the so-called 'normal', but life is meant to be experienced and explored, to be a journey of self-discovery and adventure.

The purpose of this book is to grant the reader permission to experience and celebrate the Divine in any way they feel appropriate and to do so freely, informally and spontaneously. It gives each one of us permission to sing around a blazing fire, to dance in the moonlight, and to speak from the heart. It does not seek to take away the high ground that each individual has chosen to stand on, but to simply offer another perspective from which we can explore our spirituality, both within ourselves and within the realms of nature.

How to navigate the book

The first two chapters of the book provide an introduction into the ways of the people we refer to as our 'Pagan ancestors' and to explore how their philosophy and practices have influenced modern day Pagan beliefs and the now accepted cycle of seasonal celebrations.

The main body of the book, however, has been woven into a specific pattern, with each festival having subsections designed to engage the reader in didactic, experiential and experimental learning, whilst simultaneously transporting them to a world of mystery and magic.

MRS DARLEY'S PAGAN WHISPERS

A brief overview of each festival is outlined at the beginning of each chapter with relevant dates, alternate names and any closely associated festivals. Following on from this is a larger section, which details the origins of each festival, how it was once celebrated and the folklore that has become associated with it throughout the ages.

The seasonal tales are thought-provoking stories, which describe some of the experiences I encountered during my first year in Cornwall. All involve my once next-door neighbour, Mrs Darley, a delightfully eloquent, yet mysterious lady of a certain age, and a selection of her enlightening and often eccentric friends, the most memorable of whom was Phyllis, a lady of some seventy years, for whom I always held a certain degree of affection. From each experience I was privileged to share with these people, I learned a little about spirituality, a certain amount about life, and much more about myself.

'Celebrating the festivals' provides an insight into how Mrs Darley encouraged us all to become involved in each occasion and hopefully offers ideas on how to mark each occasion in the home or in nature. These ideas are definitely not Celtic or Neolithic in origin, nor are they meant in any way to portray how our ancestors celebrated their festivals. They are merely suggestions of how modern day followers of the seasonal wheel can invite the essence of the changing seasons into their lives.

The penultimate section of each festival reflects on the thoughts and emotions many of us experience as the year progresses. This aims to give the reader permission to feel as they do. My work as a Meridian Psychotherapist and Clinical Hypnotherapist has taught me that people often feel guilty about the way they feel or think and many do not realise that seasonal changes can have a profound effect on the psyche. This is most often seen through the manifestation of Seasonal Affective Disorder (SAD), due to the lack of natural daylight, or even festive stress, something that we probably all suffer from! That said, this section does not encourage feelings of self-pity or self-degradation, but encourages positive action and forward movement.

The final section offers suggestions for a simple dedication, which can be performed inside or out with minimal preparation. The words of course can, and should, at some point be replaced with your own heartfelt prose or poetry.

I hope this book will become a treasured friend and companion as you journey along the seasonal path, a friend gentle enough to guide you and yet loving enough to encourage you to spread your wings.

Chapter 1

A Whisper of Yesterday

The spiritual history of Britain is largely unknown, which makes the tantalising remnants of the past even more mysterious and appealing. Our ancient and sometimes brooding landscape is dotted with stone circles, dolmen, cairns, barrows, quoits, standing stones and burial chambers, which span millennia, from the tombs and long barrows of the early Neolithic period (circa 5000 to 3800 BC) to the stone circles and round barrows of the late Neolithic period some 1500 years later. Although constructed thousands of years apart, many of these substantial monuments act as enticing bridges to the past and, although we can never be certain of their exact purpose or usage, they excite the imagination and encourage us to weave our own tales of magic and mystery.

Today, the turning wheel of the year, with which this book is primarily concerned, and its eight recognised modern festivals, is often referred to as being of Celtic origin, circa 1000 BC, up to and including the Roman occupation from 43AD to 400 AD. As a result, the word 'Celt' or 'Celtic' has become synonymous with the mystical and magical. We imagine the Celts to have been an enigmatic race and one to which many people living in these islands today still wish to be associated. It brings to mind artists and poets, musicians and healers, magicians and prophets, Gods and Goddesses, and a strong connection to the earth and her natural rhythm.

In truth, however, only four of the festivals celebrated by today's followers of the seasonal wheel can definitely be attributed to the Irish and Scottish Celts, these being the quarter festivals of Imbolc, Lughnasadh, Beltane and Samhain, with the latter two being of the greatest importance. The purpose of these festivals was to mark out the seasons and the beginning and end points of the agricultural year. The Celts do not appear to have been too concerned with the movement of the sun and therefore did not formally celebrate the astronomical festivals as far as we can be aware, namely the solstices and the equinoxes, although some references are made to summer bonfires.

Disappointing? Initially yes, but upon closer inspection the mysteries deepen, for the origins of the solstice celebrations appear to have their roots firmly planted in the late Neolithic period and several stone circles and tombs are aligned to the rising or setting sun at this these particular times of year. A few are also aligned to the equinoxes, although formal celebrations of these festivals are attributed to the later Anglo Saxons. The question has to be asked as to why these solar celebrations all but disappeared between the Neolithic and Anglo Saxon times, a span of some 2000 years?

One of several reasons suggested by Professor Ronald Hutton in his book, *The Pagan Religions of the Ancient British Isles, Their Nature and Legacy* (1993), is that between 1400 and 700 BC the climate in Britain changed quite dramatically, becoming cooler and wetter, resulting in the top soil of large areas of cleared woodland being washed away, leaving in its wake moorland, peat bogs and marshland. This meant that many people and tribes abandoned their original settlements and moved elsewhere. Coupled with this was a serious volcanic eruption in Iceland, which deposited ash over northern Scotland and blocked out the sunlight, thus forcing large numbers of people further south.

Perhaps this goes some way to explaining why the building of stone monuments appears to have stopped from 1500 BC and there is little evidence of even the existing monuments being used from 1200 BC onwards. The people we refer to as the Celts, therefore, were not privy to the rituals and celebrations of their ancestors some 300 to 500 years previously and gradually the marking of the sun lost its importance and appeal for the native people of Britain.

MRS DARLEY'S PAGAN WHISPERS

Today, however, followers of many differing Pagan paths celebrate and acknowledge both the agricultural festivals of the Celts and the solar festivals of the Neolithic peoples, the latter being re-introduced with the arrival of the Anglo Saxons in the fifth and sixth centuries. Rather than remaining pure in either their Celtic or Neolithic nature, however, these seasonal celebrations have become entwined with the cultures and beliefs of many invaders to these islands over the past 2500 years, including many modern contributions made during the twentieth century, resulting in a rich, vibrant, spiritual and cultural history.

It is now time to meet the people who left their mark upon our spiritual heritage and have an understanding of who they were, what contributions they made and how can we weave a few strands of their ancient spiritual wisdom into our own tapestry of life.

The Celts

We must begin by looking at the peoples who inhabited these islands between 3000 and 1500 years ago, generally referred to as 'The Celts' although, as we will see, this term is not as straightforward as it may seem.

The early Celts had no tradition of written records and our main source of knowledge comes from three distinctive avenues. The first comes from Greek and Roman literature, which was written at a time when much of the Celtic world was changing and is somewhat tenuous, as many well known writers of the day such as Discorides, Strabo and Caesar often relied upon third parties for their information. Their writings were also somewhat biased, for although both the Roman and Greek writers saw Britain as being at the very edge of civilization, their ultimate goal was to conquer and rule in order to have access to its rich source of minerals, such as copper and tin. The Romans, therefore, stated that the native Britons were *'barbarians with unacceptable religious beliefs'*, words which were used to justify the savage warfare unleashed upon them in 43 A.D.

Carole Carlton

Our second source of knowledge concerning Celtic society and beliefs comes from the early Christian monks, whose writings were made at the tail end of the Celtic period; however, they were written with a Christian slant and, as a result, are not a true reflection of earlier Celtic practices and beliefs.

In addition to these writings, our third source has come through archeological finds, including pieces of Celtic art, which have left us a small but useful Celtic legacy.

Up until the last two decades of the twentieth century, it was widely accepted that the Celts, referred to as 'The Keltoi' by the Greeks, were a distinctive band of people who were recognisable in Central Europe around 800 BC, mainly due to their beautiful art and craft work, their distinct language pattern, which still survives today in the Gaelic, Cornish, Welsh and Breton tongue, and their unique spiritual beliefs. It was considered possible, however, that they began evolving as an identifiable race thousands of years previous to this and had their roots in the early European Neolithic farmers of 5000 BC.

By 400 BC it was thought that these peoples were regarded as one of the four great peripheral nations of the known world and in 387 BC they were attributed with taking the city of Rome. From here they entered Greece in 279 BC, plundered the sacred temple at Delphi and continued their journey through Western Europe into France, which was then known as Gaul, and onward into Spain. It was then generally accepted that the 'invasion' of the Celtic peoples crossed the channel in three waves to penetrate both mainland Britain and Ireland.

In more recent times, however, many historians have come to the conclusion that the Celts were not so much a race of interlopers from Europe, but that the arrival of the Celts in Britain was a gradual process, born out of a slow introduction of cultural changes. These changes were brought about by the native Britons themselves, through their dealings with the European Celts when trading and also a certain amount of natural immigration from the continent. Inevitably this meant that Celtic spiritual beliefs and rituals gradually began to have an influence on daily life in these

18

islands, notwithstanding that the Welsh and the Irish in particular already had their own distinctive spiritual culture. This resulted in many of the ancient Deities of the native Britons being gradually absorbed into this new culture, providing us with what we would term today as 'Celtic spirituality'.

The basis of Celtic beliefs lay in the reverence of the land and the sacredness of nature, interwoven with a powerful feminine presence. That is not to say that the masculine principle was forgotten but, as all life derived from the mother, it was to her that particular reverence was given. She was seen as the bringer of life, death, sexuality and love.

The Celts saw the whole of nature as being alive and recognised a Divine presence in forests and streams, in mountains and caverns, and within each living thing that roamed the earth. They saw the Divine feminine in the rounded hills, secret underground caverns and the gentle waxing and waning of the moon, whilst the masculine principle was recognised in the magnificence of the stag and the heat and strength of the sun. To the Celts, nature and the Divine were one.

Their beliefs acknowledged Deities who were present in the here and now, surrounding them in their natural habitat and communing with them through the weather and the harvests, rather than a remote God who resided elsewhere. In the main, their Deities encompassed Gods and Goddesses of the sun and sky, fertility, hunting, war, death, the underworld, water and healing.

This is not to say that the Celts were a beautiful people who were soft and fluffy, far from it! For the Celts were never afraid to spill blood and today we may look upon them as quite a barbaric people about which much has been written. Writers such as Strabo (63 BC to 21 AD) and Caesar (circa 50 AD), considered the Celts to have rather strange spiritual practices and, although in the main these were tolerated, comments were made about the more obscene rites of head hunting, human sacrifice, and divination by ritual murder.

The beliefs and culture of the Celts cannot be looked at

seriously without mentioning the infamous Celtic priesthood, the Druids. Before the Roman invasion, the Druids held a powerful position in Celtic society both in Britain and Gaul, and were described by Irish sources as being soothsayers, prophets and magicians. Caesar tells us that the Druids officiated at the worship of the Gods, oversaw sacrifices and gave rulings on religious matters. The majority of the ceremonies and sacrifices were conducted in sacred tree-lined groves, and undertaken on specific days of the moon's cycle to ensure an auspicious outcome. Contrary to popular belief, however, very few sacrifices were made to appease the Gods; rather, they were carried out for the purpose of divination, where the future was predicted according to the death throws and positioning of the entrails of the unfortunate victim. The writings of Caesar can be verified on this topic, by several examples of archaeological sacrificial rites dating back to this period, including that of Lindow man.

The Celtic people nevertheless had a strong spiritual culture where much importance was placed upon the acknowledgment and celebration of the changing face of nature and specific agricultural events, in particular the lambing season (Imbolc), the beginning of summer when the animals were driven out to pasture (Beltane), the gathering of the first harvest (Lughnasadh), and the beginning of winter when the animals were brought in from pasture (Samhain). Therefore no matter how distasteful we may find some of their practices today, the Celts were far more 'connected' to a Divine presence than perhaps we are as a nation in these modern times.

The Romans

When the Romans finally invaded Britain in 43 AD, having had to abort two earlier attempts due to the Roman armies being needed elsewhere in Europe, they too brought with them their own spiritual culture of classical Gods and Goddesses which they had, in turn, adopted from their Greek neighbours. In addition to their Deities, the Romans introduced many of their own festivals, such as Sol Invictus, the festival of the invincible sun, held at the darkest time of year in December and Lupercalia, held in February, the month of purification.

The Romans, however, were far less intent on forcing their spiritual beliefs on the Britons, than imposing upon them those of a political and military persuasion. In fact, they appear to have been reasonably accommodating with regards to the beliefs of the native Celts and often worshipped at shrines dedicated to both a Celtic and the Roman Deity, who not only had different names but also had very different responsibilities and powers.

An example of this can still be seen today at the Roman baths in the city of Bath, where originally the Celts built a huge shrine dedicated to their Goddess Sul, or Sulis, and called it Aquae Sulis, a place where hot healing springs bubbled up from the earth. Sulis was the dark Celtic Goddess of prophecy and the underworld, and today there are many examples of curses on display in the Roman Baths Museum, written on lead plaques by the people of the day. They would then cast these plaques into the steaming waters in the hope that the Goddess would look upon their request in a favourable light.

When the Romans came along they also wished to worship at the shrine, but their chosen Deity was Minerva, Goddess of wisdom and crafts. However, in acknowledgement of Bath being an original Celtic shrine, the name of the Celtic Goddess was allowed to rank first in any inscriptions, and many artifacts are inscribed with the name of 'Sulis Minerva'.

Roman rule was not accepted willingly by the Celtic Britons, which resulted in many rebellions and uprisings during the first 100 years of occupation. The most famous of these was the sacking of the Roman city of Londinium by Queen Boudicca, leader of the Celtic tribe known as the Iceni. She gathered together an army of some 100,000 men, women and children following the rape of her daughters and her own public flogging by the Roman governors, and marched on Londinium. Sadly, however, Boudicca and her army eventually succumbed to mass slaughter and enforced slavery by the unstoppable machine that was the Roman army.

Being wise to the possibility of similar uprisings, the Romans discovered that the Druids, who occupied a sanctuary on the Isle of Anglesey (then called Mona), were affording protection to certain rebellion leaders and so made the decision to destroy the rebels and the Druids simultaneously. The confrontation between the Druids and the Roman troops was described by the Roman writer Tacitus, who told of wild haired women in black robes, waving torches, whilst the Druids lifted their hands to the sky and screamed dreadful curses. So intimidating was the scene that the Roman soldiers had to be forced forward by their leader Suetonius in order to put the Druids and their company to the sword, to ensure that *'their barbarous superstitions'* could no longer be practiced.

The Anglo Saxons

In 410 AD the Romans finally left Britain, and soon the native tribes began petty infighting. Being so engrossed in their task, the defence of the country was of secondary importance and soon small skirmishes began to take place on the eastern coast between the natives and various tribes from Northern Europe including the Picts, Jutes, Franks, Angles and Saxons. Many of the latter group had often worked in Britain under Roman rule, but with the Romans gone, they saw an opportunity to invade and take control.

There is evidence in many parts of England that the Celts eventually succumbed to Saxon rule and lived side by side with them, although they were seen as being of a lower class. Many historians, however, claim that the Saxons forced the native Celts into the far west and north of the country, which is where we consider the 'Celtic' people of today to be, namely in Ireland, the Isle of Man, Scotland, Wales and Cornwall, with many still attempting to maintain their own special cultures and beliefs.

The Saxons, like the Celts, lived in a world which was filled with magic. The Saxon poem 'Beowulf' provides us with many stories of the time, whilst a manuscript called 'Lacnunga' documents many magical herbs and plants which were used for healing. The Saxons had a strong belief in what we might consider today to be 'magical beings'; dragons and elves, sprites and giants, witches and wizards all of which had their place in Saxon society. Watery places, forests, mountains and caves were entrances to other worlds, and the eyes of the Gods were everywhere. It was a time of prophecy and divination, where nothing of importance was left to chance; the phases of the moon, omens and visions of the seers were part and parcel of everyday life.

The Saxons acknowledged two of the great Celtic festivals: Samhain, which they called Hallowe'en, which heralded the beginning of winter, and Beltane, which marked the beginning of summer. In addition, they also saw midsummer as being of magical importance for, like many before, they believed the veil between the worlds was thinnest on these three occasions. According to the writings of the Venerable Bede, however, the Saxons also appear to have celebrated the winter solstice, albeit on the 24th December, which they called 'Mondranicht' or 'The night of the Mother', an occasion they acknowledged as being of the highest sacred importance. He also mentions the Spring Festival of 'Eostre' the Saxon fertility Goddess, as ranking high on the ladder of celebratory rites.

The Saxons also brought their own Deities, with Woden (equivalent to the Norse Odin, the Roman God Mercury and the Celtic God Lugh) being the most important and after whom Wednesday takes its name. In addition to their Gods, they also had a belief in 'Wyrd' or fate (equivalent to the Greek Moirai or the Norse Nornir), which wove its thread through all those who walked the earthly plane and was generally acknowledged to be greater than all the Deities.

Gradually, however, the influence of Christianity began to make its mark on both the Saxon and Celtic way of life, with some areas becoming more prone to its influences than others and was only briefly interrupted by the re-introduction of Pagan beliefs and ideas when the Vikings came to call in 780 AD.

Christianity

Christianity finally made its way to these islands during the fourth century AD, following the conversion of the Emperor Constantine in 312 AD. It was not, however, readily accepted and was both banned and restored in England many times during the next hundred and fifty years. Nevertheless, there still remained a few staunch Pagan strongholds in Ireland, The Isle of Man, Wales, Scotland and Cornwall, all of which managed to practice their long held beliefs until the latter part of the sixth century. In 597 AD, Pope Gregory the Great sent an official mission from Rome to bring Christianity to the British Isles once and for all, and slowly the new religion began to win its long battle against the Pagan structure which had held sway for so long.

Acknowledging that winning the native Britons over to a new religion would not be easy, the Christian church attempted to both appease the people and minimise the confusion of dates and festivals, by either overlaying the Christian festivals upon the existing Pagan ones, or celebrating them within close proximity. It is from this unlikely marriage of Pagan and Christian influences that we celebrate today's accepted Christian festivals, all of which are drenched in Pagan magic, legend, folklore and superstition.

With Christianity taking quite a firm hold throughout Britain, much of what was once held sacred by the Pagan inhabitants of these islands began to diminish. The respect and reverence once given to the female in society began a rapid decline and female Deities were no longer recognised or honoured under the new patriarchal religion. Male domination had begun, nature and animals were no longer respected or revered, and the practice of natural healing arts, such as herbalism, was seen as witchcraft. The sacred act of sex and its depiction in art and literature was seen as evil and much of it destroyed in the name of the church.

For all its hard work, however, the church was aware that Paganism still had its followers and the confusion of mistaking witchcraft with Paganism (something which still exists today in many areas of society) led to the horrendous witch hunts of the fifteenth century, a practice which continued for 300 years until the mid 1700s.

The majority of those put to death for supposedly being a 'witch' or dabbling in the dark arts were either people who were not popular with their neighbours, or harmless women and occasionally men, who were simply seen as witches due to them being well versed in the practice of herbalism or natural healing, all of which the church condemned as being evil. Anyone could be accused of witchcraft and for a variety of reasons, which ranged from the failure of the crops to the sickness of a child. With no one to come to their defence, these so called 'witches' were often sentenced to death by hanging, although in Scotland burning was often a preferred method of execution.

In 1736 the 'Witchcraft Act' was passed, which strangely did not condemn witches to death, but merely stated that as witchcraft and magic did not exist then no one could practice it! It forbade anyone to accuse another of the crime and anyone doing so, or who was seen to practice in public, was merely sentenced to a year in prison.

So the Christian faith that the majority of the population now generally accept and hardly question became the formal religion of these islands but, for many deep within the stillness of a forest glade or a mountain glen, the sacred earth lay still and waited.

The Vikings

In the late eighth century another set of invasions began to take place, but this time it was the Vikings who settled in various areas of Britain, namely Northern and Eastern Ireland, South Wales, the South East coast of England, and across Yorkshire to the West and North coast of Scotland.

The Anglo Saxon Chronicles record the Viking attacks as taking place intermittently from 780 AD until the arrival of the Normans from France in 1066. The Vikings were Norsemen, of Danish, Swedish, Norwegian and Icelandic descent; they were strong warriors, who initially had little respect for the indigenous peoples of Britain or their property.

They did, however, have very similar beliefs to those of the Saxons, having once been their close neighbours and celebrated the same festivals but had, up until arriving in Britain, escaped the influence of Christianity. Their arrival therefore brought a temporary revival of Paganism, through their Norse Gods and Goddesses such as Frigga and Odin, and specific divination methods of Runic carvings.

Very soon, however, they succumbed to the influence of a mainly Christianised Britain and their beliefs, like those of the races before them, were all but lost.

The Present

Life is so fast today; we work, fly around the world, look after families and socialise, often to the detriment of giving any thought to our spiritual essence. Everything is about physical survival and making that survival as materially comfortable as we possibly can. After all, none of us want to live as our Celtic, Roman or Saxon ancestors did, but perhaps the price we have paid for our clean and convenient lifestyles has been too great.

Quality time spent with family and friends is often sacrificed, as we have to work long hours to survive financially. The art of conversation and intimacy has all but disappeared, replaced by the TV, DVD, computers and play stations. Home cooked nutritious food has virtually vanished in preference to microwave dinners, takeaways and ready meals. On a global scale we are experiencing strange weather patterns, unaccountable pollution and waste, simply because of our 'need' to race around the planet in modes of transport which cause high emissions of carbon monoxide or to have everything pre-packaged in indestructible wrapping to appease our convenient lifestyles. Most importantly, however, many of us have lost our spiritual connection, our personal relationship with the natural world and have become out of sync with her natural rhythm.

It is very difficult, especially during the cold dark nights of winter, when we are cosy, warm and well fed, to think of what certain times of year meant to our ancestors. Had their harvest been good enough to carry them through another harsh winter? Would the older members of the community survive the cold weather ahead? Supermarkets and the NHS were millennia away!

Our ancestors understood the earth's natural cycles as their lives were closely entwined with nature and her unpredictable moods. They spoke her language and communed with her through the rhythm of drums, songs, fire, water, plants, imagery and perfume, especially when the seasons were about to change, or when there was a major agricultural event such as harvesting or taking the animals out to pasture. Gradually these times were celebrated with festivals, eight of which are now marked by festivals, eight of which are now venerated by many modern day Pagans, whilst several albeit unknowingly, are celebrated by the majority of the population within a Christian context.

No matter how hard we try to block out these natural rhythms and dismiss them as unimportant in our modern, stress-filled lives, we are part of nature and, although we may deny it on a conscious level, subconsciously we cannot help but feel the pull of her magnetic force.

Many people today are turning towards a more nature-based spirituality and moving further away from patriarchal doctrines, which have held sway for some 2000 years. Upon this spiritual path there is choice; choice to follow a lone path or work with others; choice to follow a particular branch of Paganism such as Wicca, or the Norse tradition; or to follow a more eclectic path. Whichever route the journey takes, it is all about forming a personal relationship and connection to a Sacred or Divine essence.

It is important to point out, however, that whatever the belief structure of an individual, the natural cycle of the year can be incorporated within any existing spiritual practice. The turning wheel does not deny the existence of a God, Goddess or Divine presence, but celebrates it. Therefore, by adopting our ancestors' reverence for nature and acknowledging the Divine in everything,

Carole Carlton

it can only enhance or compliment any existing belief structure.

Naturally in today's society, we would not wish to revert back to the more barbaric practices of our ancestors and, therefore, much of what is written and celebrated today has been somewhat sanitised. Much of this was carried out during the twentieth century, where set agricultural and astronomical festivals were marked on the modern Pagan calendar for those who wished to follow the turning wheel of the year. Since that time, what we now perceive and accept as the umbrella term of 'Paganism' has become more and more popular as a spiritual practice or focus.

It now becomes easy to appreciate that the beliefs of our ancestors are as diverse as they themselves were and that 'ancient spirituality' as we perceive it today is an eclectic mix of Neolithic, native Welsh, Scottish and Irish traditions, European Celt, Saxon, Ancient Greek, Roman, Norse, and Christianity. All these traditions have become interwoven to produce a wonderfully exciting and vibrant spiritual heritage, a heritage of which we should be proud and willing to embrace fully, rather than deny or be selective about any particular part.

Chapter 2

Spinning the Wheel

Pagan paths, of which there are many, more often than not, are based upon an acknowledgement of a Divine presence within nature, as acknowledged by the pre-Christian peoples of these Islands and Northern Europe more than 1500 years ago.

To celebrate and honour this Divine presence, many modern Pagans follow what is popularly termed as 'The Wheel of the Year', a seasonal cycle of eight (sometimes nine, if Twelfth Night is seen as separate) festivals, celebrated at key points throughout the year, usually approximately six to seven weeks apart. These festivals include the four agricultural festivals Imbolc, Beltane, Lughnasadh and Samhain, as celebrated by the Irish, Scottish and sometimes Welsh Celts, and the four astronomical festivals being the summer and winter solstices and the spring and autumn equinoxes, thought to be celebrated by the Neolithic peoples of these islands and also the later Anglo Saxons.

As the wheel travels along its seasonal path, it shows us differing aspects of the Divine feminine and masculine forces in nature. The soft undulations of the earth, watery caverns, and the changing cycle of the moon represent the feminine, whilst the male is seen in the foliage of the woods, the waxing and waning of the sun, and the power of the stag.

The wheel brings into our awareness a pattern of birth, sacred union, death and rebirth; symbolised by the interaction between the God and Goddess as they continue their fateful journey throughout the year.

In the seasonal journey we are about to undertake, the feminine aspect of nature is symbolised by the earth as it journeys from seeding to germination, from blossoming to fruit, and finally from decay to rest. The earth therefore becomes personified as the

Carole Carlton

Goddess in her three forms of maiden, mother and crone. The Maiden emerges as the earth gently awakens in the spring and prepares for the miraculous process of seeding and germination. The Mother blooms in summer, radiant in her pregnancy, as she pours out her love upon the earth to provide flower and fruit. Finally, the Wise Crone brings decay and rest to the earth as winter approaches, a necessary part of the sacred whole before the cycle spirals once again towards a renewed Maiden earth.

The masculine aspect of the cycle is seen in the waxing and waning of the sun's strength, personified as the God, from his welcome return at the winter solstice to his sacred springtime union with the earth as he coaxes her to germinate and seed. From his glorious peak at Midsummer when the earth flowers and fruits beneath his touch, to his sacrifice and gradual decline as the earth turns to slumber, and autumn turns to winter in readiness for his solstice rebirth.

So now, as the Maiden form of the Goddess whispers to us of hope and new beginnings at the festival of Imbolc, it is on a cold February morning that you are invited to step onto the 'Wheel of the Year.'

Chapter 3

The Festival of Imbolc (Imbolg or Oimelc)

(Otherwise known as The Festival of the Goddess Bride (St Brigid's Night) or Candlemas in the Christian calendar.)

Imbolc or St Brigid's Night celebrated Sundown 1st February to Sundown 2nd February. Candlemas celebrated 2nd February.

The festival of Imbolc speaks of hope and renewal, of anticipation and longing. It is the very first festival following the darkest time of year, and the growing light between dawn and dusk brings a feeling of freedom as the first whisper of early spring caresses our senses. Newborn lambs adorn the fields, bringing a certain softness to the hard edge of winter and we gradually become aware that this is a time of powerful transformation. Beautiful snowdrops break through the hard crust of iced earth, illustrating that strength and stamina can be found within the most delicate of nature's creations and, we are reminded that although the earth may be dressed in a soft blanket of snow, or dusted with an icing suger frost, the magic of nature is beginning to awaken and stir beneath our feet.

Having given birth to her son at the winter solstice, the Goddess now releases her Crone/Mother aspect and takes on the face of the beautiful maiden, metaphorically illustrating to us that the earth is beginning to stir after her winter slumber and that the first signs of fresh, new life are becoming apparent.The God meanwhile, is now a pubescent male, who was released back to the land of the mortal at the festival of Twelfth Night in January. For the moment, he roams the earth, enjoying his freedom and is content to seek the earthly pleasures of youth, ultimately however, he awaits the hand of fate to lead him into the arms of the Goddesss at the next festival.

Carole Carlton

The Return

Deep within the earth she sleeps,
Dreaming dreams of her awakening.

Deep within the earth she calls,
The snowdrops from their slumber.

Deep within the earth she breathes,
The frosted breath of morning.

Deep within our soul she lights
The spark, which sets us free.

Festival Origins, History and Myth

'Can you feel it, dear?'

I looked up from my snow clearing, spade in hand and was greeted by the strange sight of Mrs Darley, standing barefoot in the newly fallen snow.

I nodded, 'It is rather chilly.'

'Not the temperature, dear,' she said, 'the movement, can you feel the movement?'

I must have offered a blank look as my reply.

'Beneath your feet: the movement beneath your feet.'

Moles briefly came to mind, but were instantly dismissed as Mrs Darley bent down and cleared a patch of snow with her hand. 'Look,' she said.

I creaked through the virgin snow to where her attention was focussed and noticed the appearance of tiny green shoots breaking the earth's surface.

'She's coming.' She whispered knowingly.

'Who?' I whispered in return.

'The Goddess,' she said.

Unsure of my reply, I simply nodded and smiled as Mrs Darley tiptoed lightly back to her open cottage door.

MRS DARLEY'S PAGAN WHISPERS

Imbolc

I have since learned that although the festival of Imbolc was far less romantic and far more practical to our Celtic ancestors than the initial image portrayed to me by Mrs Darley, it was no less magical, for it marked the beginning of the lambing season which to the Celts meant the difference between survival and extinction.

The word 'Imbolc' (pronounced Im – olc) actually means 'in the belly'; and in the belly of the earth, the stirrings of Mother Nature begin. An alternative term is the word 'Oimelc', which means 'the first flowing of the ewe's milk', both of which are appropriate terms for this exciting time of year.

Festival of the Goddess Bride or St Brigid

The festival of Imbolc was once the festival of the benevolent and beloved Irish Celtic Goddess Bride (pronounced Breed), who was later Christianised as Saint Brigid.

Bride was not only revered by the Irish themselves, but also by many European cultures who knew her by the various names of Brighde, Bridget, Brigid, Brighid, Brid, Brig and Brigantia (the latter having given its name to the Celtic Kingdom in the north of England) whose name means 'Exalted one'.

Bride is often depicted as the transformed gentle maiden Goddess, who is symbolic of the festival of Imbolc. This image, however, actually belies her true nature and tenth century Irish writings provide us with a far more accurate description when they say that Bride was, *'The daughter of Daghda, the great God of Tuatha de Danann, a woman of wisdom'*.

The Tuatha de Danann were said to be a race of Divine beings, which inhabited Ireland long before the time of the Celts. Bride therefore came from good stock and was indeed a woman of wisdom, often depicted as a triple Goddess, in that she was patron of Healers, Smiths and Poets.

She was, some say, brought up as a wizard and was adept at both prophecy and divination and acquired the enviable skills of

33

being able to multiply both food and drink, including turning her bath water into wine!

She was the Goddess of light and it was thought that her special domain within the house was that of the hearth and fire. She presided over the ale harvest and the earth's abundance in general and had a close association with livestock and animals, often portrayed in art with the wolf, snake, ox, boar and birds of prey.

She was also the patron Saint of virgins, and therefore was said to look after brides on their wedding day. Interestingly, the word 'virgin' in those days did not mean 'a woman who had not had sex' as we understand it today, but referred to a woman who had sexual encounters, yet belonged to no man and was therefore 'possessed only by herself'. In ancient times the priestesses of the temples of the Goddess were referred to as 'virgins', engaging in sexual relationships, but not solely committing themselves to any one man.

In contrast, expectant mothers called upon Bride during childbirth as she was looked upon as a guardian of children, often being depicted with her arms full of gifts for them.

It comes as little surprise to discover that a Goddess who was held so dear in the hearts of the Celts should be embraced and Christianised by the early Christian church, and so the Goddess Bride became St Brigid, and in Ireland was second only in popularity to St Patrick.

In Celtic times the chief shrine to the Goddess Bride was at Kildare and a group of women known as 'the daughters of fire' always tended the shrine to ensure that the flame that burned in her honour remained alight.

When Bride became Christianised, we are told that St Brigid became abbess of the convent at Kildare. The fire traversed the religious divide, for within the convent burned a fire, which had lasted for more than a thousand years; it never died and never increased in ashes. We are told of this miraculous fire in the writings of Gerald of Wales when he visited the abbey in the twelfth century in which he described a ritual involving twenty nuns.

Each night for nineteen nights, one of the nuns would watch over the fire, whilst on the twentieth night the nun on duty would fetch logs and place them beside the fire, saying 'Brigid guard your fire, this is your night', and then leave. In the morning the logs would be burned and the fire would still be alight.

In the thirteenth century, however, the papal envoy of London ordered that the fire be put out but, according to the records of the time, the local people were furious and ordered the Bishop to have it relit. The flame therefore continued to burn until the reformation when, under the orders of Henry VIII, it was finally extinguished.

It is easy to see how the myths and legends which built up around the Goddess Bride became entwined with Christian doctrine and there is one source which tells of St Brigid's ale harvest being so abundant that enough ale was made to serve seventeen churches!

To those who lived in Ireland as late as the beginning of the eighteenth century, Brigid's night would still have been a very important occasion. The belief was that the Saint would visit the most moral of houses and bless all those within as they lay sleeping. It was most important that food was left out for Brigid and that Brigid's cross was made and hung above the door or window as a sign of welcome. The crosses were then generally left up for a year, after which time the old one was burned in favour of the new.

Brigid's cross is an off-centre cross, woven out of rushes or straw, similar in design to the swastika, which in itself is said to date back to prehistoric times. Indeed, Janet and Stewart Farrar quote from the Irish Times in 1977, which suggested that the cross was: *'Probably derived from an ancient pre Christian ceremony connected with the preparation of the seed grain for growing in the spring'*.

On the eve of the festival, women in many households throughout Ireland, the Isle of Man and the Hebrides would make Brigid's bed. This bed was lovingly decorated with ribbons and stones, into which they would place a doll made from oat sheaves and cloth. Into the bed was also placed a phallic symbol of some kind, such as a stick or wand of birch, ash or hazel, as this represented the male principal. This symbolism employed a form of sympathetic magic, to encourage male and female forces to enter the home and provide a fruitful year for the family. The ashes of the fire were then smoothed over and a candle lit beside the bed. Just before the women of the house retired for the night they would call into the night three times from the doorstep, 'Bride is come, Bride is welcome'.

Next morning would reveal whether the home had been favoured by a visit from Brigid. If there was either the impression of her footsteps or the mark of the phallic wand in the ashes, then the household knew they had been favoured and could either expect a good harvest or an increase in their family or flock during the year. If nothing appeared, the family would bury a cockerel (a sacred bird to the Celts) where three streams met, as an appeasement to their Goddess.

Candlemas

The date of 2nd February is also synonymous with the Christian festival of Candlemas, the date upon which, according to biblical records, Mary went to the temple to undertake a purification ceremony forty days after the birth of her son.

The origins of the word, however, are uncertain. The only (loose) explanation stems from the Gospel of St Luke where, upon Mary's arrival at the temple for her purification ceremony, she was greeted by the Gentile Simeon and his wife, who acknowledged Jesus as 'a light for revelation to the Gentiles'. However, it seems to have taken some time for a candlelit procession to have become associated with this ceremony and it was not until the writings of the Venerable Bede, around the end of the eighth century, that the use of candles in a Candlemas procession are mentioned for the first time.

At this ceremony, Mary would have been expected to make an

animal sacrifice, of either a pair of doves or two pigeons, in order to cleanse her of the sin of having sex and especially for giving birth to a male.

In medieval times this act of purification caused theologians some concern, as they could not explain why, if Mary was a virgin, she would need to be cleansed of the sin of having sex; however, they finally decided that Mary was simply abiding by the Jewish law of the time.

Other closely associated festivals

In Rome, February had always been recognised as a month of purification and its name derived from the Roman word 'februa' meaning 'purification'. Indeed the Roman festival of Lupercalia was held on 15th February, which involved the priests of the God, Pan, racing through the streets and whipping women with goat skin thongs as an act of purification and fertility.

Holy Wells

The Bronze and Iron Age peoples saw water as having supernatural powers whilst its dark mysterious depths were seen as the gateway to the underworld. People felt compelled to make offerings to the Deities, which they believed inhabited these magical places, as evidenced by many archaeological finds including jewellery, plaques, coins and both animal and human remains. No doubt these were the original 'wishing wells' that we throw our small change into today, in the hope that the spirit of the place will grant our heart's desire!

Wells were also seen as places of healing, of communing with the Gods, of worship, of purification and divination. There was however a darker side to some requests from these watery places, as findings from the Roman shrine of Sulis Minerva in Bath disclose, through the discovery of plaques inscribed with curses and hexes.

Many Holy wells in Ireland are dedicated to St Brigid, but

Scotland too has watery shrines dedicated to this popular Saint. At St Brigid's well in Grampian, as late as 1860 an event was recorded which told of a group of women dancing naked around the well, whilst an aged woman stood in the centre and sprinkled water over them to sweep away their bareness. Another story from the same well tells of brides visiting the well the day before their wedding to ensure they would be fertile enough to bear children.

Wells eventually became Christianised in the late eleventh century due to the amount of importance placed upon them by the general population. The church made proclamations against all magical activity being carried out at any well and stated that, until each well had been blessed by a bishop and placed under the domain of a Saint, no one was allowed to visit them. Cannon Anslem stated in 1102, *'Let no one attribute reverence or sanctity to a fountain without the Bishop's authority'*.

Cornwall offers us many examples of wells now dedicated to Saints, although many of them are thought to be pre Christian in origin. The oldest known is at St Cleer on the south eastern edge of Bodmin Moor, although the original structure has long since been replaced.

In later times 'Well Dressing' became popular and, although its origins are unclear, it is presumed that it is a later continuation of the Celtic practice of making offerings to the Gods.

There is written evidence of Tissington well in Derbyshire being dressed for the first time back in 1350 as a thanksgiving by local people that they had escaped the plague. Indeed, although half the population of Derbyshire died in the plague, the inhabitants of Tissington remained untouched due, it was thought, to the purity of the water from the well.

Well dressing today can of course involve the whole community in anything from floral displays to holding a church service and is very popular at this time of year. Apart from the formal group rituals of well dressing, however, many may prefer a more solitary pilgrimage to leave a token of their choice and it is often commonplace today to see strips of ribbon or cloth hanging from tree branches which are close to a holy well, as an offering to its Spirit, Saint, or Deity.

Evidence of this can be seen at Madron well in the far west of Cornwall. It has been suggested that this tradition may have stemmed from the legend of St Helen's well in Rudgate, where the spirit of the well would only accept offerings of pieces of young girls' clothing!

Spring Cleaning

The origins of spring-cleaning are firmly rooted in this particular time of year. Our ancestors wished to ensure that there was absolutely nothing left over from the winter solstice celebrations by thoroughly cleaning the house from top to bottom and ceremoniously burning anything remotely connected to the Yuletide festival. Today, however, most modern homes ensure that nothing remains of the Christmas decorations after Twelfth Night. This early ritual spring clean was seen as a safeguard against a haunting or visitations from beyond the veil during the coming year. The house would then be ready to welcome in the spring.

Sacred Imbolc Plants

Everyone looks for the first snowdrop as proof that our part of the earth is once more turning towards the sun, but folklore maintains that we should be wary of bringing them into the house before St Valentine's Day as any unmarried females could well remain spinsters! Farming tales are also rife with snowdrop superstition, for it is said that any hens that are sitting when snowdrops are brought into the house will not lay and that the milk from the cows will be thin and the butter colourless!

Snowdrops symbolise the return of the maiden and for all their delicate appearance are strong and independent, both of which are necessary qualities for these first flowers, which appear above the earth to face the harsh winter weather.

Carole Carlton

An Imbolc Tale

One cold late January morning as I was on my way to work, I met Mrs Darley returning from her daily ritual of tipping out the ashes from her fire around the back of the old pig sties.

'Ah,' she said, 'I'm glad I've seen you. Phyllis and I will be dressing Martha's well on Saturday at sunrise.'

I raised an eyebrow quizzically.

'It's Imbolc, festival of the maiden,' she said, obviously hoping that would explain everything. 'We always do well dressing at Imbolc, in honour of Bride, the Irish Goddess.'

'So who's Martha?' I asked.

'Martha used to live at number 3, some 30 years ago, and continued to use the well on the moor long after a water supply had been brought up here. A woman of nature one might say. To be truthful, I don't know which saint the well is dedicated to, so we call it Martha's well and honour the Goddess Bride. It seems to work quite well,' she answered thoughtfully. 'Oh by the way, white and green are the colours of the day.'

With this parting comment she disappeared and I was left to contemplate this forthcoming event on my way to work.

Saturday morning brought an Imbolc gift of thick fog, as our select company of three set off onto the rain-sodden moor.

'Here we are,' said Mrs Darley, as the well appeared before us after a ten minute climb.

She immediately began to unwrap a joint offering from Phyllis and herself of an ivy swag interwoven with white ribbons and laid it across the lintel of the well. I followed suit but with a far more modest bunch of pine branches and silver honesty.

'Drinks, dear?' Mrs Darley looked at Phyllis, who right on cue produced three paper cups from her bag and filled them with whiskey from a hip flask.

My obvious doubtful look at having to drink whiskey so early in the morning was brushed aside with a wave of Mrs Darley's hand.

'It's for the Goddess dear…Oh, and it will keep you warm,'

she added as an after thought. 'These damp foggy mornings can get on your chest'.

She turned to the East and raised her cup.

'To the maiden Goddess, whose beauty springs forth from the barren earth, we honour and thank you. To Bride.'

'To Bride,' said Phyllis.

'To Bride,' I echoed.

We all drank our chest-warming whiskey and stood for a moment in silence. What a strange scene we must have made, standing there on the misty moor like Shakespeare's Weird Sisters upon the heath.

The moment was broken by Phyllis, unwrapping a small parcel, which contained four pieces of cold buttered toast, onto which she scooped a portion of scrambled egg from a thermos flask.

'Now we can feast,' she said.

'Why four pieces?' I asked.

'One for Bride,' she said as she placed the toast carefully upon the lintel. 'It is a sacred act to share food between friends.'

I smiled, and knew that both Bride and Martha would appreciate this simple yet meaningful gesture made in the pale grey light of an Imbolc dawn.

Celebrating Imbolc

This is a time of new beginnings, as the first signs of life begin to enter our awareness and can be celebrated in many ways.

At Imbolc, I remember Mrs Darley's cottage looking rather like a scene from an ice maiden's palace. It was dressed with white throws, candles and vases full of silver honesty, picked and dried in the previous autumn, whilst in the centre of the deep sill stood a magnificent statue of a bird of prey, one of Bride's totem animals.

On the Sunday afternoon following Imbolc, Mrs Darley invited Phyllis, Rose and me to join her in a 'creative crafts day', in honour of the Goddess Bride. Here we were given free reign to paint, draw, play music, write, sew or embroider. The only condition of entry into the cottage was a 'fee', payable in food for the bird table at a time when many birds are hungry.

Tea was the order of the day, neat for the hardened drinker or containing a tot of whiskey for those who liked it watered down! Throughout the afternoon, the wonderful aroma of rosemary wafted throughout the cottage and I later discovered that Mrs Darley sprinkled the dried herb on her grill pan and, with the grill on a low heat, it scented the whole cottage, bringing a feeling of warmth and security to us all.

Imbolc Reflections

At this cold and seemingly unending part of winter, we often feel tired and depressed, longing for the time when the sharp frosts give way to spring sunshine and its warmth begins to penetrate our lives once more.

From the cold hand of winter, however, the lambs are born, from a barren earth snowdrops burst for freedom and deep within each one of us lies the potential for rebirth.

As the Goddess returns in her maiden form, Imbolc offers us a time to look at the world with new eyes and recapture opportunities that we perhaps felt were lost to us. It may be time to rekindle strained relationships, or to train for a career which has always appealed, but for which we felt too old or under qualified. Imbolc offers us a second chance. It wipes the slate clean and gives us permission to feel young again, but at the same time advises us not to totally sacrifice the wisdom we have gained in favour of youth.

Shaking off winter ailments can be a problem, so perhaps beginning a new health regime or making time for regular relaxation will help us feel rejuvenated in order to greet the maiden.

At this time of year many people feel ready to step onto a new spiritual path, or to revisit a path that once felt comfortable but that they have since neglected. Traditionally this was a time when the priestesses of the Goddess undertook their initiations and made a commitment to their chosen Deity.

This is the ideal moment to resurrect New Year resolutions made (and possibly lapsed) in January. It is always difficult to maintain promises that are made in the cold dark days of January when there are so many seasonal left-overs to tempt us away from our diets or exercise routines. In February, however, when our thoughts are a little closer to spring, those resolutions may be easier to keep!

Cleansing and clearing are two words which suit the essence of Imbolc, as this is February, the Roman month of purification. This can be a cleansing of the self, in undertaking a good 'detox', or a clearing and cleansing of the home, in keeping with the tradition of spring-cleaning. It can of course be something far more substantial such as moving away from people with whom we no longer feel comfortable. This ensures that our lives have room for welcoming in the new as the year moves forward.

Interestingly, an old Irish tradition was that husband and wives were allowed to leave each other at Imbolc, a custom which persisted into the twelfth century, long after Ireland actually became Christian.

Imbolc beckons us to move forward into the new year, feeling freer and lighter.

Imbolc Dedication

Find somewhere you will not be disturbed, burn essential oils or incense of your choice and play music if you wish. Take into the room a drink (alcoholic or otherwise), something light to eat, a lighter or matches and one or more white candle(s).

When you feel ready, dim the lights and light your candle(s).

Now still your mind for a moment or two and become aware of the aroma you have chosen to burn. When you are ready, you may use the dedication below to address Bride, or your chosen Deity, or of course you may wish to write your own. When you have finished, raise a glass to toast the occasion and have something to eat to ground yourself. When you blow out the candles, ask that the energy be sent to somewhere it is needed, rather than direct its path yourself.

Failte leat a Bhrid

(This simply means 'Welcome Bridget' and is pronounced 'Falche lai a Breed')

Welcome Bride
Lady of wisdom.

Welcome Bride
Lady of healing.

Welcome Bride
Lady of prophecy.

Welcome Bride
Lady of light.

Welcome Bride
Lady of plenty.

Welcome Bride
Lady of poets.

Failte leat a Bhrid!

The Snow Maiden

In the darkness I come
And wrap myself around you,
Assured that when you wake
You will gaze in wonder at my virginal beauty.

MRS DARLEY'S PAGAN WHISPERS

Lose yourself in my softness,
Feel me yield beneath your touch,
Will me to stay,
Yet know it cannot be
For the warmth of your embrace
Will lead to my eternal sacrifice
And in an instant I will be gone,

Possessed only by myself.

Chapter 4

The Festival of the Spring Equinox

(Or the Feast of Ostara or Eostre, in close proximity to Easter and Lady Day (The Annunciation) in the Christian Calendar.)

Spring equinox: celebrated according to astrological alignment, between 20th to 23rd March.
Feast of Ostara or Eostre: celebrated anytime between 22nd March and 19th April, dependant upon the moon.
Easter: celebrated anytime between 22nd March and 25th April, dependant upon the moon.
The Annunciation or Lady Day: celebrated on 25th March.

The festival of the spring equinox speaks of freshness and youth, of excitement and endless possibilities. Nature begins to quicken and early flowers open to the warmth of the strengthening sun, bringing the colours of lemon and yellow into our lives on the wings of a March wind.

This is the first time during the year when day and night are of equal length, but from this day until the summer solstice daylight hours will increase as we journey onward into summer.

The God and Goddess meet and fall in love. They seal their meeting by making love and the Goddess becomes pregnant.

The Binding

Fresh on the wings
Of a March wind
You run…

Wild and free

Carole Carlton

Yet, bound,
With knowing
Yet, unsure.

Feel the blood of life
Coursing through your veins.
Feel the animal passion
Rising in your loins.

Run, run, wild and free
For She is but a whisper away…

Know
That when you gaze upon her face,
Her beauty will bind
And your destiny beckon.

Festival Origins, History and Myth

I looked up and waved as I saw Phyllis emerging from the door of
Mrs Darley's cottage carrying a stunning arrangement of
daffodils.

'How beautiful,' I said, genuinely impressed.

'Hogarth's curve, dear,' said Mrs Darley over Phyllis's
shoulder. 'Mind you, they say you need uniform flowers to really
do it justice, but the thing about Mother nature is that she doesn't
do uniform, she simply does unique and that's much more
interesting.'

I nodded, appreciating the wisdom of her words.

'Yellow is the colour of early spring,' she said, 'just look at
your garden!' She gestured towards the borders, which were full
of primulas, crocuses and daffodils. 'The most cheerful of
colours,' she continued, 'almost reflective in its nature and it is of
course the colour of the mind.'

'That's why we surround ourselves with it!' laughed Phyllis,
'in the hope that its properties will rub off.'

MRS DARLEY'S PAGAN WHISPERS

'Nonsense dear,' said Mrs Darley dismissively, 'Yellow light simply encourages us to think more positively. It lifts our spirits and raises our self-esteem in time for summer.'

I immediately made a mental note to surround myself with the colour of the season and, like Phyllis, hoped that some of its properties would rub off on me.

The Spring Equinox

There is little evidence of the equinoxes being celebrated by our Celtic ancestors, due to the fact that they were more interested in marking the beginning of each season or significant agricultural events.

The people of the Neolithic era, however, appear to have acknowledged the equinoxes in certain parts of the British Isles, as can be evidenced from the passage tombs at Knowth (circa 3200 BC) in County Meath, where one passage is aligned with the equinox sunrise and the other with sunset.

The spring equinox, however, brings a degree of uniformity to the wheel of the year and is important in its own right on three counts. Firstly it acts as the mid-point marker of the sun's journey from winter through to summer; secondly, it has been essential in the calculation of the Christian festival of Easter for centuries; thirdly, it coincides with the sowing of many crops as the new season begins. Whatever its origins and meaning to our ancestors, it is certainly a time worth acknowledgement by modern followers of the seasonal wheel.

The word 'equinox' simply means 'of equal length' and refers to the twelve hours of daylight and twelve hours of darkness at this point in the year. It was originally thought to stem from two Latin words *aequus* meaning equal and *nox* meaning night. The word 'Vernal', as this equinox is often called, is derived from the Latin word *vernus* meaning 'of spring'.

Easter and the Feast of Ostara or Eostre

Carole Carlton

The Christian festival of Easter is celebrated in close proximity to the time of the spring equinox and, although many of us are aware that it is the most important of all the Christian festivals in that it commemorates the death and resurrection of Jesus, perhaps the origins of the word 'Easter' are less well known.

In the eighth century, the Venerable Bede stated that the Christian festival of Easter was named after the month in which the festival of the Saxon fertility Goddess, Eostre or Ostara, was held, known as 'Eostur Monath'. By his own admission, however, Bede did not actually research any of these facts and we cannot, therefore, be certain as to whether this Saxon Goddess did provide us with the origins of the word Easter, or whether the source lay elsewhere. Indeed, the Saxons used the word 'Eostur' to also mean 'opening' or 'beginning', so it could simply mean 'the month of beginnings' and have little or no association with a Saxon fertility Goddess at all.

That said, there was a Greek Goddess called 'Eos', who was associated with the dawn and new beginnings, and Eostre is often considered to be a Saxon variation of Eos. Many myths and legends have built up around this Saxon Deity, some of which are outlined in this chapter.

Whether Eostre, Ostara, Eostur, or Eos, we can be certain that the word 'Easter' was derived from one of these sources.

Bede stated that the festival of the Saxon Goddess, Eostre, was celebrated on the day of the full moon following the spring equinox, which bears a certain similarity to the way in which Easter is calculated following the ruling at the council of Nicea in 325 AD, although it did not become standardised in the British Isles until the eighth century.

There is a slight difference in the calculation of Easter, however, in that it is celebrated on the *Sunday* after the first full moon (or Paschal moon to give it its authentic Jewish title, originating from the Latin word for Passover, *pashcalis*) following the spring equinox. This means that Easter can fall no earlier than 22nd March and no later than 25th April.

MRS DARLEY'S PAGAN WHISPERS

Spring Fires

Legend has it that during the festival of Eostre, all fires had to be extinguished in the Goddess' honour and could only be relit from a sacred flame in the centre of the village. The new fire was seen as a symbol of sacredness and purity, something which everyone wanted to bring into their homes at such a lovely time of year when everything was fresh and new.

The sacred fire was always kindled by rubbing wood against wood and the sparks were caught by dry chips placed in a hollow where a spindle was turned. It was believed that unless all household fires were extinguished then the new flame would not come. This custom transferred neatly over to the new religion of Christianity, although in later times the extinguishing of everyone's fires became impractical, and instead a simple fire was lit on Holy Saturday from which the Pashcal candle was lit to symbolise the resurrection of Christ.

Legend tells us that the High King of Tara, who ruled supreme over all the Kings of Ireland, looked out from his castle one day during the festival of Eostre and saw a fire blazing away on a far hillside. Furious with this obvious disregard for the law, for which the penalty was death, he sent out soldiers to arrest the guilty party. When the soldiers arrived at the hillside they found St Patrick, the patron Saint of Ireland, piling wood onto his fire and immediately seized him. Standing before the King he was asked why he disobeyed the law, and he explained that his fire was a sign that Christ had risen from the dead and was the light of the world. The King so admired Patrick's courage that he forgave him and became a convert to Christianity!

Easter bunnies and Easter Eggs

Strange as it may seem, the association of eggs and bunnies at Easter time are actually connected and, to discover more, we must once again turn our attention to the Saxon fertility Goddess, Eostre.

There is a delightful story which tells of Eostre finding an injured bird on the ground and, in order to save its life, she transformed it into a hare. The transformation however was incomplete and, although the bird looked like a hare, it still retained the ability to lay eggs. Regardless of this slight mishap, the hare was so grateful for the goddess saving her life that on Eostre's festival the hare would lay eggs, decorate them and leave them as a token of thanks. In Germany today, many young children still believe that their Easter eggs are laid and delivered by the Easter hare.

The decorating of eggs in bright colours remains a popular custom, once known as 'Pace Egging' and is thought to derive once again from the Latin word for Passover, *pashcalis*. Indeed the household accounts of Edward I in 1290 itemise the purchase of 450 eggs for 18d to be coloured and distributed amongst chosen Lords and Ladies.

Egg rolling also became a popular Easter pastime and huge crowds would gather to watch eggs being rolled down a suitable grassy slope. This is still carried out at Avenham Park in Preston, Lancashire.

Naturally, eggs have always been seen as a symbol of new beginnings and resurrection, a most appropriate symbol for this time of year, both from the Pagan and Christian viewpoint. Our Greek Goddess Eos most likely gave us the origin of the word 'oestrogen', a component essential for new life, whilst in the Christian church eggs were seen as a symbol of the resurrecting God. In Medieval times, eggs were blessed in church. Quoting a prayer sanctioned by Pope Paul V: *'Bless O Lord, we beseech Thee, this Thy creature of eggs, that it may become a wholesome sustenance to Thy faithful servants, eating in thankfulness to Thee, on account of the resurrection of our Lord.'*

Hot Cross Buns

Contrary to popular belief, the cross which dominates the hot cross bun is not a Christian symbol, as it pre dates Christianity by at least a thousand years. The Celtic Druids saw the circle as representing the eternal circle of life, and the cross contained within it represented the four elements essential for life itself, fire, earth, air and water.

In Roman times, bread and cakes were marked with a cross to symbolise the four lunar phases and were made as sacrificial offerings at the point of a crossroads to the Roman moon Goddess, Diana. The quartered cross is an ancient sign of completeness, often seen on Celtic crosses in churchyards today.

During the nineteenth century, a superstition close to people's hearts was that any bread baked on Good Friday would never go mouldy, and would protect the household in which it was hung. Breads were also said to have healing powers if consumed and be particularly beneficial for digestive disorders. To depict the crucifixion, these breads acquired a cross and became known as hot cross buns.

In the nineteenth century, however, we are informed that the previous year's bun was re-hydrated, re-baked and eaten by household members, a tradition we could all probably dispense with today in view of our 'sell by dates'!

The Annunciation or Lady Day

The Christian festival of Lady Day, or Annunciation day, falls on 25th March and commemorates the day on which the Angel Gabriel visited Mary to tell her of the forthcoming birth of her son in December. Interestingly, the spring equinox is the time that our Goddess and God meet and consummate their relationship, resulting in the Goddess also becoming pregnant with a due delivery date of the winter solstice, around 21st December.

Sacred Spring Plants

If you walk in woodland at this time of year you will probably see the delicate violet growing quite close along the edge of the path, and for this fragile gift we have to thank the Roman God Attis.

The story of Attis has a somewhat familiar theme, although it pre-dates Christianity by several hundred years.

Attis was born of a human virgin called Nana, and sacrificed his own life to save mankind. He was crucified on a pine tree and, where his blood spilled onto the earth, violets were said to have sprung.

These flowers are often seen as a symbol of both sacrifice and regeneration and are also said to protect against evil spirits, and calm frayed nerves, encouraging peaceful sleep.

If a love potion is in order, then combining lavender and violets seems to be an irresistible recipe! It is worth remembering, however, that violets are a protected species and perhaps the essential oil of violet leaf and lavender would make suitable substitutes, therefore leaving the flowers in their natural habitat.

Daffodils, often referred to as the 'Lent Lilly', and primroses abound at this time of year and both are blessed with the ability to attract love, although the primrose is now also a protected species. A vase of daffodils in the bedroom is said to assist with conception difficulties, although the minimum number in a vase should be thirteen! Visit the daffodil fields in Cornwall, a feast for the senses!

This is the time to plant seeds, although they should be kept indoors or in a greenhouse until the frosts have gone. These will not only adorn your patio or garden in the summer but will be symbolic of new beginnings as spring enters your life. Bless the seeds as you plant them and visualise them growing into a strong and healthy plant.

Planting herbs is also a recommended springtime activity to use in summer salads, to preserve to last the winter, or for simply losing yourself in their beautiful aroma. It has always been traditional, according to old gardening lore, to plant parsley on Good Friday between the hours of 12 and 3 when, it is said, the devil is otherwise occupied!

Discovering The Green Man and the Horned God

Although symbolic of the sun, the God at this time of year is often symbolised as the 'Green Man', a foliate face of leaves and greenery. He can be found in ceramic masks, in the cornices of old buildings and in the pew and pulpit carvings of old churches. Kilpeck Church in Herefordshire is an excellent example of this.

The Green Man has also become synonymous with Cernunnos, the Celtic horned God, often portrayed in Celtic art as part man, part stag, who roams the greenwood wild and free. He is a character of strength and power, but often sadly mistaken for the devil by the Christian fraternity due to his horned appearance.

It was thought that the Celtic God Cernunnous was once worshipped in the royal forest, and some have seen a horned figure on horseback riding through the woods followed by a pack of hounds.

We know of Cernunnos (whose name literally means, 'horned one' or 'peaked one') from a stone altar discovered beneath Notre Dame in Paris, which depicts the head and shoulders of a bearded man who bears the ears of a stag and a set of antlers, upon which are hung two torcs. Above the head the name Cernunnos appears in Roman letters.

Horned figures, however, stretch back into antiquity. The Minotaur is a famous example of a horned beast, which was half bull, half man, whilst the mischievous and lustful Roman God Pan was depicted as being half man, half goat. Ancient Egypt was no exception, as the Goddess Hathor was portrayed with cow horns whilst Osiris, God of the underworld, bore the horns of fertility.

Horned humans are not unknown to medical science as there is a rare skin disease, which goes by the name of 'Cornu Cutaneum', a cutaneous growth, which resembles a horn and grows from the scalp.

A Spring Equinox Tale

The spring equinox celebration included a dawn trip to the nearby Rillaton Barrow, a Bronze Age burial mound high up on the

Cheesewring Moor, with its entrance facing directly east.

'A great archaeological find, dear,' Mrs Darley informed me, rather breathlessly, as we climbed up to the entrance. 'A skeleton, dagger and gold cup were all found here. However, the gold cup ended up in the royal bathroom for some considerable time until the death of George V and now stands in the British Museum, although you can see a copy of it in Truro if you wish. Come,' she said, patting the top of the lintel, 'we'll sit here a while and wait for the sun.'

The sun duly arrived in all its spring glory over the eastern horizon, bringing a golden glow to the swathes of mist, which hung in the fields between Dartmoor and Bodmin.

'Delightful,' said Mrs Darley. 'But time to make a move, I said we would meet Phyllis and Rose at the Hurlers stone circles for light refreshments at seven o'clock.'

I presumed (correctly) that 'light refreshments' would include a tot of whiskey, but was pleasantly surprised for this to be accompanied by a home made Cornish Pasty, still slightly warm from Rose's oven.

'Equinox greetings dears!' called Mrs Darley, as we made our way to the northern most circle of the Hurlers standing stones.

Having been warmly greeted by Phyllis and Rose, we sat on a waterproof sheet draped over one of the fallen stones and ate our early morning feast.

'What's the history of the Hurlers?' I asked.

'Supposedly men and women were playing the game of hurling on a Sunday and so were turned to stone by God,' explained Phyllis.

'Complete poppy cock though,' chimed in Mrs Darley, 'these stone circles pre date Christianity by thousands of years! No one really knows why they were built, as is the case with most of these monuments. Perhaps it's best left that way…more for us to muse over.' She added thoughtfully.

I suddenly glanced at my watch. 'Oh, I thought it was later than that,' I said. 'It's only ten past eight.'

'I make it quarter to nine,' said Rose.

'My watch must have stopped then,' I said. 'That's strange, I put a new battery in it only last week. Ah well, I'll take it back on Monday.'

'There will be no need,' said Mrs Darley mysteriously, 'your watch will work perfectly well when you leave the Hurlers. Come let us acknowledge our Lord and Lady.

We all turned to face the east and the brilliant sun, which was rising rapidly in the morning sky.

'All hail to the growing sun and its union with our sacred mother,' said Mrs Darley.

'To the union,' we chanted, raising our paper cups of whiskey to the sun and taking a drink before pouring a little out upon the earth.

Once back at Mrs Darley's cottage, I glanced at my watch and was surprised to see it working once again, albeit an hour slow. 'It's working!' I stated, pointing to my wrist.

'Why of course it is dear, its workings are merely affected by the power of the granite. Time matters not. It is but an illusion. The past and future are merely human perceptions. Real time is now, in this eternal moment. Likewise the sun is always at the full height of its power, it is only our perception which makes it appear weak or strong, according to where we stand upon the earth.'

I wrestled with this information as I made my way back home and gradually came to realise that the only way we can improve our lives or make changes is by taking action now, in this very moment, and that personal perception is what colours each of our lives a different shade.

Celebrating the Spring Equinox:

This is a time of forward movement, as the March wind blows away the last traces of winter.

On the Sunday before the spring equinox, Mrs Darley had a tradition of inviting the local children, which during my time included Rose's daughter Lucy and her cousin Joshua, round to the summerhouse for a morning of egg decorating and rolling. Naturally the children had to be supervised and so at least half a dozen adults (including me) would also squeeze ourselves into the summer house to make and decorate our hard boiled eggs with poster paints and glitter, whilst also enjoying home made hot cross buns or 'Celtic buns' as Mrs Darley liked to call them.

Just before lunch the eggs were laid out on the table and Black Bill, who lived alone in an isolated cottage on the other side of Sharp Tor, came round to judge them and then stayed on to join Mrs Darley and Phyllis for lunch.

The prize of a chocolate Easter egg was presented for the best one and this was followed by egg rolling down the field below the cottage gardens. The winner of this second competition got to keep the decorated eggs in order that they may leave them outside their homes on the day of the full moon following the spring equinox, to bring good luck as they honoured the Goddess Eostre at her festival.

Spring Equinox Reflections

The time for thinking and incubating ideas is over, as the spring equinox heralds a time of 'doing', a time to begin putting all those well-laid plans into action. This beautiful time of year calls for movement, both in the way we think and the way we act. It encourages once shadowy ideas, to grow into something more tangible that we are able to carry forward into the awaiting spring. It encourages us to initiate conversations, make telephone calls and write letters enabling the ideas that were sown in the dark days of winter to germinate and grow.

We should mirror the initial meeting of the God and Goddess and make new contacts or consider renewing old ones, echoing the theme of resurrection which threads its way through the Pagan and Christian world alike.

The equinox brings us into the present moment and within that moment all potential is held. It is important to view each second as a precious gift and use it wisely to enrich our lives and the

MRS DARLEY'S PAGAN WHISPERS

lives of those around us.

Spring Equinox Dedication

Find somewhere you will not be disturbed, burn essential oils or incense of your choice and play music if you wish. Take into the room a drink (alcoholic or otherwise), something light to eat, a lighter or matches and one or more candles of yellow or lemon to represent the spring sunshine (white will always suffice if you do not have coloured candles).

When you feel ready, dim the lights and light your candle(s).

Now still your mind for a moment or two and become aware of the aroma you have chosen to burn. When you are ready, you may use the dedication below to address the Goddess and give thanks for her gifts or, of course, you may wish to write your own. When you have finished, raise a glass to toast the occasion and have something to eat to ground yourself. When you blow out the candles, ask that the energy from the flame be sent somewhere it is needed rather than direct its path yourself.

<u>Gifts</u>

From the heartbeat of anticipation
To the slow ache of longing.
These are the gifts of the Goddess.

From the richness of passion
To the heaven of ecstasy.
These are the gifts of the Goddess.

From the warmth of friendship
To the presence of love.
These are the gifts of the Goddess.

Lady, we thank and honour you.

59

Carole Carlton

<u>Springtime</u>

Call to me
As the leaves burst for freedom,
Fly to me
As a bird on the wing,
Run to me
As the sun starts to strengthen,
Come to me
On a whisper of spring.

Dance with me
On a hill dressed in moonlight,
Swim with me
In the wild open sea,
Ride with me
Through the white mists of morning,
Drink of me
And set yourself free.

Chapter 5

The Festival of Beltane

(Or May Day, or Roodmas in the medieval Christian calendar.)

Beltane: celebrated Sunset 30th April to Sunset 1st May.
May Day and Roodmas: celebrated 1st May.

As the Celtic summer dawns with the first breath of a May morning, the festival of Beltane whispers to us of magic and bewitchment, of vibrancy and passion, where Mother Nature pulsates with life and the human heart beats to the rhythm of her drum. The strengthening sun invites us to shed a few layers of clothing and we instinctively respond as our whole being becomes lighter, brighter and more joyful.

May is one of the most beautiful months of the year, full of excitement, opportunity and endless possibilities. It probably comes as little surprise, then, that this is a time for experiencing the many facets of love, as we allow ourselves to become seduced by the intoxicating festival of Beltane.

With the Goddess carrying the child of the Green Lord, they celebrate and seal their sacred union by marrying beneath the May. This festival depicts the Goddess in her duel role of maiden and mother, albeit from now on the maiden role will diminish. The God also realises and acknowledges the commitment he is about to make, as he too bids farewell to his carefree existence and takes on the serious role of the Goddess' consort.

The Wedding

Sweet hangs her scent
On the first breath of morning,

Carole Carlton

Soft drapes her gown
In the first light of day,
Come now my Lady
The Green Lord is waiting,
Waiting to wed his Queen of the May.

Proudly he stands
In the shade of the Greenwood,
Awaiting her coming
As she walks his way,
Come now my Lady
The Green Lord is waiting,
Waiting to wed his Queen of the May.

United they kneel
In the first rays of sunlight,
Their destiny sealed
As fate weaves her thread,
Come now my Lady
The Green Lord is waiting,
Waiting…

Festival Origins, History, and Myth

Unable to sleep due to work pressures, I found myself sitting on the cane chair in the porch with a steaming cup of coffee, just as dawn was breaking on a cool but beautiful late April morning. I plugged the little electric heater into the lounge socket and dragged it out into the porch to warm my bare legs and prepared to watch the sun rise.

My thoughts, however, soon blotted out any intention of watching the wonders of nature as sales targets, appointments and an impending review filled my head. Just as quickly as the thoughts came, however, they were dismissed by a loud knock on the window behind my head. I spun round, coffee dancing through the air.

'Morning dear,' waved Mrs Darley. 'I saw you sitting and wondered what brought you up so early.'

'Couldn't sleep,' I said, 'and anyway I have to be in work early for a meeting.'

Mrs Darley nodded and made her way back to her own cottage. I noticed that she was wearing a wrap and walking boots and wondered where she had been so early.

I was just considering going for a shower, when she reappeared at the porch door with a tray in her hands.

'You'll need this,' she said, 'to nourish your body for the day ahead. It's porridge with honey and a little something special.' She turned to leave. 'Oh, and that,' she said, pointing towards the eastern sunrise, 'will nourish your soul, if you just take a moment to drink it in. The Celtic summer will soon be upon us, perhaps it is time to banish the cold dark thoughts of winter, which haunt you and let the sun enter your life. Magic abounds, my dear, use it wisely.'

Beltane, Roodmas and May Day

The word 'Beltane' is derived from the Irish Gaelic 'Bealtain', or the Scottish equivalent 'Bealtuinn', the meaning of which has two possibilities. The first, found in tenth century texts, derives from two words, 'Bel-fire', meaning bright, lucky or goodly fire, which refers to the great fires made by the Druids through which they drove their cattle before sending them out to pasture. The second suggestion is that it was named after a Northern European God called 'Bel' or 'Belenus', to whom two sacred fires were lit at his festival. Whichever account is the more factual; Beltane heralded the beginning of summer for the ancient Celts.

'Roodmas', meaning 'the mass of the cross', was the name given to Beltane by the Medieval Christian church. The church fathers wished to stamp out the common people's allegiance to the lusty may pole, a symbol of life and fertility, and replace it with allegiance to the cross, a symbol of suffering and death.

May Day has become the modern term for Beltane, with the

word 'May' being derived from Goddess Maia, originally a Greek mountain nymph, who was later honoured as the most beautiful star of the constellation of the Pleiades.

The Beltane Fire

On May Eve in Ireland and Scotland, Beltane fires were lit on the highest hilltops up until the mid 1800s. Welsh literature, however, only provides us with very sparse details regarding a similar fire festival, although the day itself was singled out as a special day and was known as 'Calan Mai', the day upon which two Welsh dragons always fought each other. Within England, Beltane does not appear to have been a significant date, apart from Cumbria and the far South West, where records exist of Beltane fires.

The fires themselves had both symbolic and practical aspects. Symbolically the fire was beneficial for many reasons. The first of which was as a form of sympathetic magic, to encourage the sun to shine and warm the crops, therefore ensuring a good harvest.

Secondly, leaping over the Beltane fire was symbolic of taking the fire within oneself to bring new beginnings. For those who had just experienced a greenwood marriage, jumping the fire was thought to bring them good luck, whilst those looking for love would jump the fire to encourage a special person into their life. Travellers jumped the fire to ensure a safe journey, and pregnant women (with some assistance) would jump it to ensure a safe delivery.

A third symbolic reason for the Beltane fires was that of protection especially, it seems, from witches. In the late nineteenth century in Scotland, fires were lit by the majority of farmers which were then run around by the younger family members who would shout, 'Fire blaze and burn the witches', whilst in the Isle of Man, residents would set fire to the gorse bushes as it was thought that this was a place in which witches took refuge.

Finally, on a symbolic level, Beltane was an agricultural

festival and as such this was the time when the cattle were driven out to pasture. Before they were allowed to go, however, the Druid priests would drive them between two Beltane fires in a magical ritual of fertility to ensure their good health and a high milk yield.

On a practical level, the animals were driven between the two fires in order to smoke the parasites from their hides which had lain there all winter, thereby ensuring they were clean and healthy for the summer to come.

Love, lust and sexuality

The festival of Beltane marked the beginning of the Celtic summer and, as such, it was a time when life was celebrated in many ways, including love making when the gift of sexual union was enjoyed and celebrated.

Many love chases were made through the woods on May Eve which, we must remember, was eleven days later than it is today due to the calendar changes of 1752 and, therefore, was probably somewhat warmer! This lusty occasion was often referred to as 'Going a Maying'. Here lovers would sometimes spend the whole night in the woods, enjoying the freedom that this festival brought, and finally returning home with flowers and garlands with which to greet the May sunrise. Relationships formed in this way were referred to as 'Greenwood Marriages'.

The Puritan writer, Phillip Stubbs is quoted as saying: '*I have heard it credibly reported by men of great gravity, credit and reputation, that of fortie three score maids going to the woods over night, there have scarcely the third part of them returned home again undefiled.*'

It is said that even after the introduction of the marriage rites as we now know them, the rules were still relaxed on May Eve and couples would venture into the woods in order to carry out whatever came naturally to them. The children of May marriages were often called after the spirits or legendary characters of the woods. Jackson, after 'Jack in the Green' a derivation of 'The

Carole Carlton

Green Man', Hodson, after 'Hod', a woodland sprite, or
Robinson, after Robin Goodfellow (Shakespeare's Midsummer
Night's Dream) or Robin Hood, the famous inhabitant of
Sherwood Forest. A seventeenth century writer tells us:

> *'Thus the robin and the thrush,*
> *Musicke make in every bush.*
> *While they charm their pretty notes*
> *Young men hurle up maidens cotes.*

Records tell us that in 1515, Henry VIII went 'A Maying' in
the company of his first wife, Katherine of Aragon, and certain
Lords and Ladies of the time, up Shooters Hill, although no
sexual connotation has been referred to by Stowe, the sixteenth
century writer: *'...on May day in the morning with Queen
Katharine his wife, accompanied by many Lords and Ladies, rode
a-Maying from Greenwich to the high ground of Shooter's Hill;
where, as they passed by the way, they espied a company of tall
yeomen, clothed all in green, with green hoods and with bows and
arrows, to the number of two hundred. One, being the chieftain,
was called Robin Hood, who required the King and all his
company to stay and see his men shoot.'*

Once restored to the throne in 1660, Charles II also took part in
elaborate May Day celebrations, riding around Hyde Park in
decorative coaches. In this royal parade were certain ladies
whom, we are told, bared their necks, shoulders and breasts to
entice the horsemen of the day!

Rudyard Kipling captured the essence of Beltane when
he wrote:

> *'Oh do not tell the priest of our art,*
> *Or he would call it a sin;*
> *But we shall be out in the woods all night,*
> *A-conjuring summer in!'*

Legend has it that long before Guinevere fell in love with Sir

Lancelot, she had many amorous liaisons. One May Day, whilst King Arthur was at war, Guinevere went 'A Maying' in the company of her maids in the Greenwood but, unknown to her, Melwas (sometimes referred to as 'Sir Mellyagraunce'), a Scottish Prince and one of her former lovers, disguised himself as the 'Lord of the Green' and frightened her maids away. He then captured Guinevere (although one text does state that she went with him quite willingly!) and took her to Scotland, from where she had to be rescued by either Sir Lancelot or King Arthur, according to differing versions of the tale.

Bringing in the May

For those who were, perhaps, not so sexually inclined, there was the opportunity to set out in small groups before dawn to greet the first light with drums or cow horns and then to gather greenery from the woods with which to decorate their homes or villages in honour of the Goddess.

The type of preferred May greenery varied according to the area of the country. The Cornish seemed to prefer sycamore, whilst the Welsh gathered birch. The tree most associated with Beltane, however, is the May, or Hawthorn Tree, but it has very mixed blessings according to ancient folklore and therefore the decision of whether to cut it and bring it into the home must rest with the individual!

In Taunton it was thought to be unlucky to bring May blossom into the house, as it was believed that witches disguised themselves as Hawthorn trees. Fairy folk were also said to live beneath them and would not appreciate their home being disturbed. On May Eve in West Somerset, however, it was considered good luck to bring in the May as long as an explanation was given to the tree that its branches were being cut in honour of the Goddess.

Even today, some consider it most unlucky to cut a branch from the Hawthorn, regardless of whether it is cut on May Eve, whilst others feel it offers protection against ghosts and lightening. At all costs, it is a tree to be respected, for who knows who watches and waits beneath!

For those who wish to retain their youth and beauty, however, the following rhyme should be noted:

> *'The fair maid who, the first of May*
> *Goes to the fields at break of day*
> *And walks in the dew of the Hawthorn Tree*
> *Will then ever handsome be.'*

Indeed, this was a custom reported in the 'Morning Post' on 2nd May 1791, which stated: *'Yesterday being the 1st May, according to annual and superstitious custom, a number of persons went into the fields and bathed their faces with dew on the grass, under the idea that it would render them beautiful.'*

Whatever the individual's choice of greenery, the placing of leaves, flowers and branches around the lintels and doors was seen as protecting the home from evil.

An old manuscript from Eton, now residing in the British Museum, tells us that the boys were allowed to rise at 4.00am on May Day to collect branches of the May tree, which were then used to decorate the school windows. The manuscript also states however that this privilege was only granted if the boys could carry out the whole task without getting their feet wet from the dew!

Flowers, wreaths and garlands were also synonymous with Beltane, as they symbolised the victory of summer over winter. 'May birching' began on May Eve when young men would make leaf and flower garlands to hang on the doorknobs of houses of various people in the village, with each type of foliage having a different meaning.

> *Those who were fair had garlands of pear*
> *Those who were glum had garlands of plum*
> *Those who had thorn were objects of scorn*
> *Those who had briar were known as a liar*

MRS DARLEY'S PAGAN WHISPERS

Those who had gorse were known to be coarse.

So the rhymes went on, often causing much upset and ill feeling, as well as delight. In the nineteenth century, May garlands were made by mothers in order for their daughters to sell on May Day, therefore bringing in welcome funds.

Dancing in the May

Dancing around the May Pole is probably one of the most well known traditions of May Day, with Welsh literature dating it back to at least the fourteenth century. Strangely it does not appear to feature in the Celtic lands of Ireland and Scotland, but was a popular sight in both England and Wales.

Maypole dancing has often been depicted as a very sexual act, with the pole representing the phallic shape of the male, and the earth into which it is placed representing the yielding feminine. In the main this is a theory suggested by the writer Thomas Hobbes, who stated that maypoles were remnants of ritual worship to the Roman God of male potency, Priapus. Other writers, however, suggest that it was merely a pole around which to dance, celebrate and hang garlands.

The dance itself often involved a certain amount of kissing, although in the main it is a round dance of alternating male and female dancers. The men dance anticlockwise, the way of death, to represent the sacrifice of the God's life, whilst the ladies dance clockwise, the way of life, to represent the eternal presence of the Goddess. Each person holds a ribbon, which forms a plait as the ribbons wind their way down to the bottom of the pole. The success of the pattern is said to indicate the abundance of the harvest the following year, whilst the energy created by the dance is said to resonate with the earth and bring about her awakening and bounty.

In 1644 the May Pole was banned by the Puritans for being far too sexual but, thankfully, was reinstated by Charles II when he returned to the throne in 1660.

Again the Puritan writer Phillip Stubbs had something to say about the whole ritual of the Maypole: *'They have twentie or fourtie yoke of oxen, every oxe havying a sweete nosegaie of flowers tyed on the tippe of his hornes and these oxen drawe home this Maie poole (this stinckying idol rather) which is covered all over with flowers and hearbes, bounde rounde abouet with stringes from the top to the bottome, and sometyme painted with variable colours, with twoo or three hundred men and women and children followying it with greate devotion. And thus being reared up, with handkerchiefes and flagges streamying on the toppe, they strawe the grounde aboute, binde greene boughes about it, sett up sommer haules, bowers and arbours, hard by it. And then fall they to banquet and feast, to leape and daunce about it, as the Heathen people did at the dedication of their idols.'*

Morris dancing is also a popular sight at this time of year and often continues well into the summer at various festivals throughout the British Isles. Philip Stubbs once more furnishes us with his observations on the Morris dance, often referred to as the 'Dance of the Devil': *'They bedeck themselves with scarves, stringes and laces hanged all over with golde rings, precious stones and other jewels: This done, they tie aboute either legge 20 or 40 belles with riche handkerchiefes in their handes, and sometyme laide across their shoulders and necks, borrowed for the moste parte of their prettie Mopsies and lovying Bessies for busying them in the darke. These thyngs sette in order, they have their hobbie horses, dragons and other antiques, together with their bawdy pipers and thunderying drummers, to stricke up the Devil's dance withal, then marche these heathen companie towards the church and churchyard, their pipers pipying, drummers thunderying, their stumps dancying, their bells jinglying, their handkerchiefs swinging about their heads like madmen, their hobbie horses and other monsters skirmishying amongst the throng: and in this sorte they go to the church dancying and swingying their handkerchiefs over their heads, in the church, like devils incarnate.'*

MRS DARLEY'S PAGAN WHISPERS

The earliest records in Britain of Morris dancing seem to date back to the fifteenth century, with a difference of opinion as to its origins. One school of thought simply suggests that it came from a court jester's dance, whilst another links it to a dance performed by Spanish Arabs, with the name being derived from the 'Moorish' people. In the early twentieth century, however, it was suggested that the dance came from an ancient fertility rite, where the masculine force was represented by the use of the phallic sticks and the feminine principal was depicted by the use of handkerchiefs and that the name Morris derived from the blackened faces of some of the dancers, which were said to simply look 'Moorish'.

The striking of the sticks are said to represent the clash of the ritual battle between summer and winter, whilst the leaps of the Morris dancers indicate to the crops how high they have to grow.

Beltane Horses

Horses, both real and those of the hobby variety, play a very important part in certain Beltane rituals. The horse is seen as representing the masculine, whilst the feminine principal is either the lady who rides the horse or the lady who becomes caught beneath the skirts of the hobbyhorse.

In Middle Medieval England, the newly crowned May Queen would ride through the city of Coventry scantily clad upon a white horse, in honour of the protest staged by Lady Godiva many centuries before. Lady Godiva was the wife of the 11th century Mercian Lord Leofric who taxed his subjects harshly and, as a token of support for her people, she rode the streets of Coventry naked in a bid to persuade her husband to lower the taxes. The celebration of this custom was seen as wicked and outrageous by the Puritans and was banned along with the May Pole.

The nursery rhyme, 'Ride a cock horse to Banbury Cross, see a white lady upon a white horse', echoes this ritual.

In Padstow in Cornwall, one of the most ancient and well

known Beltane customs is carried out every year. Two 'Obby Osses', one dressed in red and white and the other in blue and white, enter the streets from their 'stables' (local pubs) and dance through the narrow streets, accompanied by drums, accordions, teasers and virtually the whole population of the village.

The 'Oss' itself consists of a black head surrounded by a frame covered in a black oil-skin skirt. It is said that any lady who becomes caught under the skirts of the Oss will either be married or pregnant within the year. The earliest written records stem back to 1803, although many feel that the custom is far older and that it is a Pagan ritual, which has its roots in the mists of a Cornish past.

The music accompanying Padstow's 'Obby Oss' day is hypnotic and the whole experience has a certain magical quality, as the 'Padstow May Song' rings out across the harbour to welcome in the summer. These two verses of the 'night song' offer a flavour of what Beltane is all about.

'Unite and unite and let us all unite,
For summer is acome unto day,
And wither we are going we will all unite,
In the Merry morning of May.

I warn you young men everyone
For summer is acome unto day,
To go to the green-wood and fetch your May home
In the merry morning of May.

Other festivals to visit on May Day are the Hobby Horse festival in Minehead, Somerset or the 'Green Man' festival at Clun in Shropshire.

Nothing can beat the real thing, but if horse riding does not appeal then a visit to the Uffington White Horse in Oxfordshire is a seasonal alternative: a chalk figure that is carved into the chalky landscape and dates back to at least the Iron Age. Legend has it that St George slayed the dragon on Dragon's Hill, which is a flat-topped mound just below the figure of the horse.

The May Queen

It was an old custom to select an attractive young maiden to become the 'Queen of the May' at Beltane, honouring the single woman aspect of the Goddess before her forthcoming marriage to the Lord of the Green. One of the best known 'maidens' is Maid Marian, from the Robin Hood folklore tales, who represents the young Goddess, whilst Robin represents the young God as the Green Man. Maid Marian is often seen in May Day celebrations today, albeit 'she' is often a man dressed up as a woman, an attempt, according to some writers, to bring about polarity and balance between male and female.

In the Catholic tradition, similar customs exist, except that the May Queen becomes the Virgin Mary, and emphasis is placed upon chastity and purity rather than upon fertility and sexuality.

The veil between the worlds

Just as at the festivals of Mid Summer and Samhain, Beltane is a time when the veils between the worlds are at their thinnest, and is a time when spirits, fairies and elves walk abroad.

The Queen of the fairies is said to ride out upon a pure white horse, looking for mortals to lure away to her land for seven years. If you sit beneath the Hawthorn tree on May Eve, then you may hear the sound of her horses' bells as she rides by, but turn your head away if you wish to stay in the land of the mortal, for if you look upon her face, she may spirit you away!

There is a Scottish Ballard called 'Thomas the Rhymer'. Thomas was a thirteenth century prophet who chose to go to Fairyland with the Fairy Queen, but has not been seen since, even though seven years have long passed!

It was also thought that fairy children, known as 'changelings', were often substituted for those of humans during the month of May.

To protect the home against the fairy realm on May Eve, branches of Rowan were placed around the doors and windows to safeguard adults and children alike.

In Ireland it is believed that any food left over from May Eve should not be kept with a view to eating it the next day, but should be left out for the fairies.

May Marriages

It was always thought unlucky to marry in May, as the month belonged to the Goddess and any man who married during this month would fall prey to the lust and power of a woman! Other suggestions for this superstition arise from May being the month in which the Romans held their festival of 'Lemuralia', where sacrifices were made to purge each house of hostile spirits and therefore marriages were not wholly appropriate.

With the coming of Christianity, May became the month of the Virgin Mary, a time associated with chastity and purity, and therefore not the ideal time for marrying.

It has often been said that to wear green to a wedding is unlucky and, when this is coupled with a May wedding, it can spell trouble! This probably stems from an old English rhyme, which states:

'Married in May and kirked in green
Both bride and bridegroom won't long be seen.'

A more realistic explanation, however, is that as the medieval church regarded green as the colour of the fairy realms, it was not deemed to be an appropriate colour to wear and was therefore said to bring bad luck by the church elders.

Once the sacred month of the Goddess had passed, the first day of June became the most popular time for a type of trial marriage, known as a 'Hand Fasting'. These 'Hand Fastings', which lasted for a year and a day, were non binding statements of intent, where a couple could see how the relationship went before deciding whether to make a more formally binding contract. Traditionally the hands of the couple would be bound together, an exchange of words would be made and the happy couple would then jump over the broomstick to seal their promise.

The full moon in June was referred to as the 'honey moon' due to its rich honeyed colour and, as June became the most popular month for weddings, the period following marriage became known as a 'honeymoon'.

Mischievous May

Fairies abound, the Lord of the Greenwood stands tall and strong and the month of May tempts us with her delights but, although the warmth of summer whispers to us on a May morning, take care, as May can be unpredictable especially in terms of the weather.

Early frosts can still catch out the enthusiastic gardener, and although we may be lured into going out without a coat, remember the old saying: *'N'ere cast a clout 'til May be out'*.

It was often thought that this saying meant to wear your winter warmers until the beginning of June. However, other scholars have suggested that it means to keep your winter clothes on until the May blossom is out in its full glory!

A Beltane Tale

Being torn between whether to have an early night or a walk up the lane on such a beautiful evening, my dilemma was solved by a knock at the door.

'Hello dear!' It was Mrs Darley. 'We're all in the summerhouse, waiting to welcome in the summer as soon as the sun goes down and wondered if you'd like to join us. You'll need a jumper,' she called, as she returned to her garden.

I smiled to myself as she disappeared, for here was yet another strange but magical invitation into this new life I had created for myself on Bodmin Moor.

Joining Mrs Darley were Phyllis, Rose, Eddie the poacher, Peter, Bod and Don, all of whom, I surmised, were on at least their second tot of whiskey!

'Do come in dear, although it's standing room only I'm afraid. We've just gathered a few sprigs of Rowan from the tree here to place around our window ledges…you'll be wanting some too,' she said, thrusting half a dozen or so twigs into my hand. 'It's for protection. Can't be too careful when the veil's thin…mischief makers abound!'

'Sun's down in five minutes,' Eddie suddenly announced, at which point everyone vacated the summerhouse.

'Come dear,' said Mrs Darley, 'time to place the Rowan around the window ledges.'

I returned to my cottage accompanied by Phyllis and Eddie who helped me to arrange the Rowan. 'But what about protecting your homes?' I asked them. 'Don't you want to do this too?'

'Oh we made sure we did that before we came out,' explained Eddie. 'Have done for years! My Grand-Mother was a firm believer in the power of Rowan for protection. Mind you, if you're really brave you might prefer Hawthorn.'

'Oh no,' said Phyllis emphatically. 'Now that is asking for trouble, it's the sacred tree of the Beltane Goddess and even on her special night I would never take any.'

'Is Rowan acceptable then?' I asked, somewhat nervously. 'I mean, we won't be treading on anyone's toes by taking any?'

'Oh no, it's been a protective plant since time immemorial and as long as you leave an offering for the tree in return for a few of it's branches then you can be assured that it will keep you from harm,' said Phyllis rather comfortingly. 'The Irish Celts believed that each Rowan tree was guarded by a dragon because of its valuable properties, and that if you carried a piece, it would sustain you for the equivalent of nine meals, add a year to your life, and its berries would heal all wounds!'

'Some tree!' I exclaimed, placing the last piece gratefully on the doorstep.

Having completed our task, we all returned in the gathering

dusk to the summerhouse, which was ablaze with tea lights secreted safely in numerous jam jars, whilst the old pot-bellied stove threw out a welcome heat in the cool night air.

'Shhhhush, my dears, one moment,' said Mrs Darley, 'this is the beginning of our Celtic summer. We must toast the sacred marriage of the Lord and Lady.' She raised her glass. 'To the sacred marriage of the Lord and Lady!'

'To the sacred union!' we echoed.

'And now let's dance the summer in!' shouted Mrs Darley.

At this point, an old tape recorder sprang into life with a rather hypnotic tune and everyone rushed out of the summerhouse and onto the grass.

'Come along dear, join in,' called Mrs Darley, grabbing my arm as she and Eddie whirled past. 'You have to dance the summer in, it all adds to the potency!'

Initially feeling somewhat inhibited, I stiffly joined in and gradually found myself becoming freer and freer, dancing with a lightness I had not experienced since childhood. Eventually, exhausted, we collapsed onto the dew sodden grass, laughing at what we must look like with damp hair stuck across our foreheads and perspiration running down our backs.

'That was wonderful!' I exclaimed breathlessly.

'That my dear,' whispered Mrs Darley, 'is the magic of May Eve!'

Celebrating Beltane

This is a time for celebrating the gift of life, as we are called to welcome in the ancient Celtic summer.

A few days after May Day, on bank holiday Monday, Mrs Darley invited eight of us to accompany her in what she called 'May Day Merriment'. She had managed to 'secure' from Eddie the poacher, half a telegraph pole, which she asked him to erect at the bottom of her garden. When Don, Bod, Peter, Eddie, Rose, Lucy, Phyllis and I arrived, the pole had been decorated with eight pieces of coloured ribbon and we were soon ushered into place, although Phyllis insisted on being in charge of the music rather than dancing and gave her place to Mrs Darley.

The ladies were given a headdress of bluebells and cowslips and instructed to dance clockwise, passing their ribbon under the first man they met and over the second, whilst the men were given buttonholes of the same flowers and instructed to dance anticlockwise, passing their ribbon over the first lady they met and under the second. This should have resulted in a beautiful woven pattern of ribbons. However, with much merriment and confusion as to who was going where, the ribbons ended up in a rather haphazard fashion as did we!

Having occasion to go into Mrs Darley's cottage after the dancing, I was fascinated to see her lounge decorated in various types of greenery, including the Rowan branches from May Eve, and an array of green and white candles to represent the sacred marriage of the God and Goddess.

Beltane reflections

Beltane is a time of vibrancy, passion, love, joy, self expression and freedom, and what better way to celebrate this wonderful festival than to reflect on whether we have enough of these ingredients in our lives at present.

If the answer is no, then perhaps we should look to incorporate as many of the following into our lives as possible and bring a little Beltane magic into our daily existence.

- Do something everyday that makes you feel alive
- Do something everyday that fills you with pure joy
- Set yourself free from mundane tasks at least once a week
- Indulge in your real passion at least once a week
- Ensure you are open to give and receive love, whether passionate or compassionate
- Always express who you truly are

In these modern times, taking time to enjoy ourselves can seem almost frivolous, especially when there is so much to attend to in the material world, money to be earned, children, partners and parents to be looked after, shopping to be done, work to be completed, but by never allowing ourselves to experience pure joy in whatever form is right for us, we are fundamentally denying ourselves one of the main purposes of life.

This is a time of vibrancy and elation, when the God and the Goddess join in marriage thereby making a commitment to each other and, in doing so, begin a whole new life. A life that is enriched by being full of purpose, full of passion and full of joy, rather than one which makes each day mundane or a chore.

We too can begin a new life, one that brings satisfaction and enrichment, whether this is by singing, dancing, running through the waves, walking barefoot on the grass or making love under the stars. Perhaps your dreams are greater than this, or perhaps more conservative, but whatever they are, Beltane is a wonderful time for expressing who you truly are.

Beltane Dedication

Find somewhere that you will not be disturbed, burn essential oils or incense of your choice and play music if you wish. Take into the room a drink of your choice (alcoholic or otherwise) and something to eat if you wish.

When you feel ready, dim the lights and light two candles. For preference, one should be green (to represent the God) and the other white (to represent the Goddess). If you do not have coloured candles then two white candles will do just as well.

Just still your mind for a moment or two and become aware of the aroma you have chosen to burn. When you are ready, you may use the dedication below to address the God and Goddess as they join together in their sacred union, or of course you may wish to write your own. When you have finished, raise a glass to toast the occasion and have something to eat to ground yourself. When you blow out the candles, ask that the energy be sent to somewhere it is needed, rather than direct its path yourself.

Carole Carlton

The Union

From the night that yields to the dawn
To the sun who chases the moon,

Blessed is the union
Which makes the sacred whole.

From the seed that holds the grain
To the sea that caresses the shore,

Blessed is the union
Which makes the sacred whole.

From the joy and the pain of love
To the mysteries of birth and death,

Blessed is the union
Which makes the sacred whole.

To our Lord and Lady
Whose blessed union
Makes the sacred whole.

The Watcher

From beneath the thorn
I watch them come,
They dwell and sit
And sing and thrum
On days such as these.

Their gifts they hang
Upon the tree
I watch them, yet,

MRS DARLEY'S PAGAN WHISPERS

They don't see me
On days such as these.

They too give thanks
For grain and corn,
For rain and sun,
For dark and dawn,
On days such as these.

And so within
The human shell,
I see that some
Kind hearts do dwell
On days such as these.

Chapter 6

The Festival of the Summer Solstice

(In close proximity to Midsummer, or the feast of St John the Baptist in the Christian calendar.)

Summer solstice: celebrated according to astrological alignment, between 20th to 23rd June.
Midsummer and the Feast of St John the Baptist: celebrated 24th June.

The festival of the summer solstice speaks of love and light, of freedom and generosity of spirit. It is a beautiful time of year where vibrant flowers whisper to us with scented breath, forests and woodlands hang heavy in the summer's heat and our souls become enchanted with midsummer magic.

Days are long, distant horizons beckon and we often feel a wonderful sense of liberation where anything seems possible. Yet, as the longest day dawns, we become aware that, from this point, the sun will begin to diminish in strength and the Northern Hemisphere will begin its gradual spiral into darkness once again.

The God and Goddess form a perfect union with each other. The God is at the height of his power and is crowned 'Lord of the Light', whilst the Goddess pours forth her love upon a bountiful earth.

Remnants of summer

Heady Jasmine,
Dancing on the breeze of summer,
Weave your way
Into my senses

That I may know you
Amid the barren days of winter.

Heavy honeysuckle,
Hanging in the warm night air,
Wind your way
Into my dreams
That I may recall your sweetness
During winter's bitter grasp.

Fragrant rose,
Whose breath of scented laughter
Nourishes my soul.
Whisper to me
That I may remember you
When the cold hand of winter touches my heart.

Festival Origins, History and Myth

'I always feel as though the sun is reluctant to say goodnight at this time of year,' called Mrs Darley from the half stable door, as I trudged wearily round from the car complete with laptop and briefcase. 'The last vestiges of sunlight are still visible on the tors of Dartmoor.'

I thankfully dropped my bags on the path and turned to take in the view, which I know would have slipped by unnoticed had Mrs Darley not brought it to my attention. As I stood, the tips of the tors finally sank into shadow and, turning to pick up my cases, I became aware of the most beautiful aroma wafting across the evening air.

'What a lovely smell,' I said.

'Morning sunrise, dear,' said Mrs Darley, pointing towards a dusky pink rose just to the right of the cottage door. 'Phyllis gave it me two years ago.'

'It's beautiful,' I said.

'Perhaps you should stop and do this more often,' she said.

I looked at her somewhat puzzled.

'Smell the roses,' she smiled. 'We always think the good times will last forever, that we will always be young, that we will have time to do the things we dream of next week or next year. But summer, my dear, is fleeting, one drop of rain and it is washed away, one cool breath and it is gone. Remember these words when the leaves of autumn swirl around your feet,' she said, and quietly closed the door.

The Summer Solstice

Celebrations of the summer solstice pre date Celtic times, and seem to have their roots in the Neolithic period. Indeed, not only the people of Northern Europe and Briton marked the occasion but also the population of North Africa. The importance of the solstice is borne out by archaeological evidence of tombs and circles, which are aligned to both the rising and setting sun at this powerful time of year, with Stonehenge probably being the most famous.

The Callanish stones on the Isle of Lewis have a legend attached whereby local people believed that 'The Shinning One' would walk between the avenues of stones at sunrise on Midsummer's Day. It appears that whereas the majority of the solar festivals were ignored by the Iron Age peoples, the summer solstice does appear to have survived in certain areas of Briton, not only in the now recognised 'Celtic' lands but also in many parts of England itself.

The word 'solstice' simply means 'The standing still of the sun' and, at both this time of year and at the winter solstice, the sun does actually appear to stand still for a few days before, in this instance, the decrease in light becomes noticeable.

To our Celtic ancestors the summer meant long days of hard work in the fields, ensuring that the harvest would be as fruitful as possible, whilst the warmth and light nights of summer promised a certain freedom in their lifestyle.

Carole Carlton

Midsummer and the Feast of St John the Baptist
The sun seems to begin to move once again around 24th June, a date often referred to as 'Midsummer' and also the date of the Christian feast of St John the Baptist.

Strangely, we have a similar scenario following the winter solstice on or around 21st December, where the Christian festival of Christmas heralds the movement once again of the sun on 25th December.

When Christianity came to these islands, the Midsummer fires, a remnant of the Pagan past, became synonymous with St John the Baptist, as his bones were said to have been burnt by the Emperor Julian and therefore the old religion and the new melded together well at this festival.

Fire Magic

Midsummer was a time of ritualistic fires and their purposes were many fold. The fires were lit to celebrate the power of the sun, to invite good luck and fertility into the community and as a means of protection, both from unseen forces and from pestilence and disease, benefiting humans and animals alike. In areas of Brittany, the May Pole was cut down at the summer solstice to form the basis of the Midsummer fire.

In the fourteenth century in Shropshire, a monk wrote of three differing types of fire made on St John's Eve (23rd June):

- A *Bone Fire* made of clean bones and no wood (later to become our well known bonfire, although thankfully very few are made from bones today!) The smell from these fires was thought to keep dragons at bay!
- A *Wake fire* made of clean wood and no bones (to socialise by or 'wake' by)
- A *St John's Fire* made of clean wood and bones. (St John, often pronounced 'Sin-jon', is perhaps where the origin of our word 'singe' derived, meaning 'to burn superficially')

Whatever the type of fire, however, Midsummer does appear to have been a time of merrymaking. Historical records show us that Henry VIII had his own Midsummer fire in the great hall, although with the coming of the reformation these celebrations all but disappeared and those which managed to survive were only destined to last until the civil war.

By 1900 there was only one record of a Midsummer fire in England and that was held at Whalton in Northumberland, a custom, which still survives today. It is held, however, on 4th July which, according to the Julian calendar, would have been old Midsummer's eve.

The Old Cornwall Society decided during the 1920s to revive the custom of lighting fires along the Cornish peninsula, beginning in the east and moving westward as dusk approached. It is a custom which continues today and, when watched from a distance, still has the power to evoke in anyone who observes this ritual a deep connection with the earth and the ancestors.

Echoes of the Beltane Fires can be felt at Midsummer, and nineteenth century Irish records tell us that leaping over the Midsummer fires was a popular pastime, as it was thought to encourage the sun to shine throughout the summer and warm the crops. It provided an opportunity for young men to show off to the opposite sex, by leaping over the flames at their height to prove their courage, strength and agility. Once the flames had died down, any girls who wished to marry early and have many children would also jump the fire as an aid to their fertility.

Rites of protection were of great importance at this time of year for our Pagan ancestors, as transitional days such as those of the solstices and equinoxes were seen as times of potential danger. An old Irish custom from the early Christian era involved the oldest woman in the community reciting prayers and circling the solstice bonfire three times on her knees to protect the community against disease.

Another protection rite involved people lighting hazel sticks from the solstice bonfire and racing home with them as fast as possible, as the first person over the threshold would be blessed with good fortune for the coming year.

Cattle often played a part in these Midsummer fires, and in certain areas of Ireland flaming bundles of hay or straw were carried from the main fire into the fields to bless the cattle. In other areas the cattle were brought down to the Midsummer fires when the embers were glowing and, as they were driven through the smouldering ashes, their backs were singed with a burning hazel twig. In Somerset as late as 1900 it was recorded that a farmer passed a burning branch over his cattle and horses at Midsummer as the flames were said to benefit all those who were associated with them. One Cornish farmer back in 1800 went to extremes to ensure good fortune and actually sacrificed his best calf in the Midsummer flames.

Even the field benefited, as the ashes from the fire were scattered amongst the crops to ensure a good harvest.

Flaming Wheels

The European Celts often depicted the sun as a spoked wheel, which has been evidenced by archaeological finds dating back to 1300 BC. In Northern Europe the discovery of the Trundholm Chariot showed a bronze model wagon, pulled by a horse and carrying a gilded sun disc. Many spoked wheel offerings have also been found at watery shrines and in burial chambers.

This symbolic sun wheel found its way into fourth century texts, where we are told of the Pagan folk of South Western France rolling a flaming wheel down a hill towards the river and, although the timing of this ritual is not specified, written evidence is available in the fourteenth century, which associates the rolling of flaming wheels with Midsummer Eve.

On the edge of Dartmoor this custom was still being carried out in the nineteenth century and, should the wheel still be lit as it reached the stream at the bottom of the hill, then the harvest would be a fruitful one and good luck would follow.

MRS DARLEY'S PAGAN WHISPERS

Elementals and Divination

Midsummer was thought to be one of three nights when the veil between this world and the next was at its thinnest (the other two being Beltane and Samhain) and when both spirits and elementals visited our world.

There is a delightful story, which comes from the Irish town of Limmerick at the end of the nineteenth century, where a group of young girls were still sitting around the solstice fire long after the rest of the village had gone to bed. Suddenly before them stood the Irish Goddess Aine, who proceeded to ask them if they would mind hurrying their celebrations as the fairy folk were waiting to have the hill to themselves.

Due to the fact that Midsummer was designated a 'magical night', many people took the opportunity to divine the future, a practice which alarmed the Christian church, and in the twelfth century it was declared that anyone caught divining during the feast of St John the Baptist should do penance for fifteen days!

The battle of the Oak King and the Holly King

The ancient Celts recognised just two seasons, those of winter, personified by the Oak King and summer, personified by the Holly King.

At the winter solstice, when the sun gradually begins to gain in strength, the Oak King and the Holly King do battle; the former is triumphant and leads us into the summer. However, at this time of year the battle is re-enacted but now the Holly King is the victor and will wear the crown until the winter solstice, when the scenario once again will be reversed.

Summer Travel

A far cry from our summer holidays perhaps, but the ancients did put the good weather to good use by undertaking pilgrimages to sacred sites such as ancient wells or shrines dedicated to the

Gods, and would often set out in groups for several days of travel before reaching their destination.

Today our thoughts too turn to travel, with some preferring deserted beaches, some pleasure beaches, whilst others still feel the pull of sacred sites and probably often visit the same places as their ancestors such as Stonehenge, Avebury Stone Circle or any of the hundreds of Holy Wells or Stone Circles which dot the landscape of the British Isles and Europe.

Sacred Solstice Plants

Roses, sacred to the Roman Goddess Venus, are blooming in their full glory at this time of year and have been associated with love for thousands of years. It was said that Cleopatra first made love with Mark Anthony on a bed covered one inch deep in rose petals, and these fragrant flowers have been scattered at wedding ceremonies for centuries.

Much legend abounds around the colour of roses and a Mediterranean legend tells us how the red and white rose came to be. The tale introduces us to a virgin who was falsely accused of a sexual deed and sentenced to burn. Her prayers, however, were so fervent that they quenched the flames and the unburnt wood magically turned into white roses whilst the charred wood became red roses.

The Virgin Mary was said to have visited St Dominic in a vision during the latter part of the twelfth century and gave him the first rosary beads, each one scented with the perfume of roses.

If you choose to grow roses in your garden then they are said to attract fairies, whilst making a necklace from the rose hips long after the bloom as died is said to attract love to the wearer!

Other plants, too, have an important part to play at this particular time of year, when they are at the height of their flowering. The ancients, of course, did not have our modern scientific know-how when it came to overcoming infertility and had to rely on natural remedies or folklore passed down via the oral tradition. One such suggestion was to walk naked in a vegetable patch on Midsummer's Eve and pick a sprig of St John's Wort. This was a plant originally dedicated to the Scandinavian sun God Baldur (later renamed after St John the Baptist upon whose feast it blooms) and was considered to be capable of making a woman pregnant!

St John's Wort was equivalent to winter solstice greenery, as many people took it into their homes around the time of the summer solstice to protect them against evil spirits, demons, lightening, and ghosts. In fact, so effective did people think it was against evil spirits that in Italy it was known as *Cacciadiavola* meaning 'Excorcist'.

In Cornwall, the long poles which marked the boundaries of the tin mines were crowned with St John's Wort to ensure protection for the mine and its workers.

The plant was thought to have great healing properties if gathered at midnight on Midsummer's Eve, especially if it was a full moon, and one of its alternative names is 'balm of the warrior's wound'. It was also said to be capable of bringing restful sleep free from nightmares, and many young girls would sleep with a sprig of it under their pillow in the hope that it would bring sweet dreams of their future lover.

A Midsummer Tale

'There, there it is, look!' An animated Phyllis tugged at my arm and pointed to the distant mound known as Kit Hill, between the two moors of Bodmin and Dartmoor.

I stared into the dusk and felt a strange excitement, a stirring, which moved my spirit as I saw the first Midsummer's Eve fire of the Cornish peninsula burst into life. I stood, captivated by its intensity in the growing darkness, and suddenly my enthusiasm for the Midsummer barn dance, to which we were all invited, waned and I wanted to be alone to savour the magic of the hour.

I found my hostess, expressed my thanks, made my excuses and whispered to Phyllis that I was tired and was going to walk home. The strains of hoedown music became ever distant as I approached the edge of Minions Moor and began to pick my way tentatively across the uneven landscape. Eventually I sat on a lonely boulder of granite and looked across to the fire, which grew ever brighter in the diminishing light, and I wondered how the ancients must have felt and exactly what meaning they attached to this ancient ritual.

Mesmerised by the fire for some considerable time, the light was fading rapidly as I averted my gaze from Kit Hill and, although I knew I was only a mile from home, I was somewhat concerned to see how dark it had become. Looking to my left, however, I was relieved to see the familiar silhouette of the South Phoenix engine house a little way ahead.

It was at this moment I saw them. Tiny dots of lime green lights sparkled in the twilight as though stardust had been sprinkled across my path. I gazed in amazement at this fluorescent phenomenon yet, strangely, did not feel compelled to inspect the lights at close quarters. I was quite content to simply stare and wonder.

Perhaps this was a message, a spiritual experience; I felt enchanted and upon arriving home went to bed feeling quite elated.

Consulting Mrs Darley next morning about what I considered to be a magical encounter, I was given an immediate and somewhat earthly solution.

'Glow worms dear! Vary rare now but still found in a few isolated places of the British Isles. They have a relatively short 'glowing window' whilst they attract a mate, so make the most of them! Where did you see them?'

'On the moor as I walked back from the barn dance last night. I was tired, so decided to leave early.'

'Ah yes, Phyllis said you'd left and I was quite concerned. Which way did you go? You didn't walk through the copse did you?'

Something in her voice made the fingers of fear fleetingly touch my heart. The dense copse was immediately attached to the cottages and dropped down quite steeply towards the hamlet at the bottom of the moor.

'No, no I didn't, I came over the top of the moor and walked down from Minions. Why do you ask?'

She placed her hand across her lips and shook her head. 'My lips are sealed,' she said. 'All I ask is that you don't walk in the copse around Midsummer. Let's just say that you may become enchanted.'

'How wonderful!' I laughed.

'Enchantment, my dear, always has a price,' she said, and walked away.

Celebrating the Summer Solstice

The summer solstice is a time for strength and vitality for action and movement.

Just before dawn on the summer solstice, Mrs Darley would light the old barbeque in her garden and within ten minutes the whole of the hamlet was huddled around it for warmth, all eyes trained on the eastern horizon, waiting.

Mrs Darley would hand out percussion instruments to each of us, varying from maracas to drums, both authentic and home-made from old washing-up bottles full of beans to boxes and wooden spoons. Then we would drum and rattle until the sun crept over the horizon and with a loud cheer we would formally welcome the Lord of the Light. I loved this festival, full of passion and raw power.

Food, of course, formed part of the celebration and with as many toasters plugged into as many sockets as we could find, warm buttery toast drizzled with clover honey made its way from the cottages into the summerhouse. Mrs Darley always told us that it was good luck to eat honey at this particular festival, as this was a gift from the bee at their busiest time of year and as such should be appreciated and acknowledged. Most of us drank a welcome cup of tea with our toast, although Cornish mead was always on offer!

With breakfast over and, before many of us went to get ready go to work or have a sneaky hour back in bed, Mrs Darley would give each of us a silver coin, usually a five pence piece and instruct us go somewhere during the day where there was running water. She explained to us that this was an auspicious time to ask for a blessing from the Divine and that in return, just like the ancients, we should cast our coin as a token of thanks into the flowing waters and end by saluting the sun to honour both the God and Goddess.

Summer Solstice Reflections

At Midsummer we feel happier, brighter and more alive than during the dark days of winter and perhaps find it somewhat easier to be more generous or more pleasant to those around us. Look at people walking in the street, they smile and it becomes contagious. Just imagine how much brighter the dark days of winter would be if we could project that happiness into the remainder of the year as the wheel once again spirals inward.

This is a powerful time when the Goddess is radiant and the God is crowned Lord of the Light and as such is very much a time for action. If there is something you have a burning desire to do, then do it; if there is something in your life that hinders you, then change it. The sun gives us an inner strength, it motivates us to achieve, to take a chance and to live. Grasp this opportunity with thanks and use it to drive your life forward.

Make sure you get out and about, whether just taking a walk in the countryside or visiting more exotic climes. Allow yourself to wonder at Mother Nature's beauty and to give thanks for the earth upon which we are privileged to spend a certain span of time.

Just as at the winter solstice, this is a joyous occasion, but now is a time of plenty, of freedom and of light. Make sure you enjoy and celebrate with good friends.

Summer Solstice Dedication

Find somewhere you will not be disturbed, burn essential oils or incense of your choice and play music if you wish. Take into the room a drink (alcoholic or otherwise), something light to eat, a lighter or matches and one or more candles, either of orange or blue to represent the power of the sun and the deep sapphire of the sea and sky (white will always suffice if you do not have coloured candles).

When you feel ready, dim the lights and light your candle(s).

Now still your mind for a moment or two and become aware of the aroma you have chosen to burn. When you are ready, you may use the dedication below to address the God, male principal or your chosen Deity at the height of his power, or of course you may wish to write your own. When you have finished, raise a glass to toast the occasion and have something to eat to ground yourself. When you blow out the candles, ask that the energy be sent to somewhere it is needed, rather than direct its path yourself.

The Lord of Fire

To the Lord of fire,
Who dresses the earth with sunlight.

To the Lord of fire,
Who blesses the earth with warmth.

To the Lord of fire,
Who caresses his Lady with love.

To the Lord of fire,
Joyfully we honour you at the height of your power.

The Weaver

Soft shone the moon upon the casement.
Soft was her foot upon the stair.
Inviting was the greenwood in the twilight,
Oh my lovely daughter, please beware.

Carole Carlton

Beckoned, by the beauty of the sweet flute,
Beckoned, by the music of the spheres,
Beckoned, by the voices of the angels,
Beckoned on, beyond her deepest fears.

And there,
Within the moonlight,
As white as maidens milk,
Stood the weaver of sleeps dream time
In a pool of pearlised silk.

The richness of his voice he draped around her.
Enchanted tales he wove into her mind.
Slowly, like the coiling of the serpent,
In her and around her he entwined.

Charmed was she by young fools and their lovers.
Charmed more so by kings and distant lands.
Charmed was she by mermaids of the oceans
And the burning secrets of the desert sands.

Beware,
My lovely daughter,
Beware,
How long you stay,
For in listening to the Weaver,
There is a price to pay.

Eternity lay wrapped within a moment
As the face of dawn breathed fire across the sky,
Regretfully she lightly traced her footsteps
And silently she bid a sad goodbye.

Running to the pool beside the meadow
She splashed her face with water cool and clear
But as she stared into the liquid mirror

MRS DARLEY'S PAGAN WHISPERS

The vision paralysed her heart with fear.

Beware,
My lovely daughter
When you heed not what I say.
For in listening to the Weaver,
There is a price to pay.

'No, please,' she cried out at the cold reflection.
'The face that's staring back cannot be mine.'
Stolen was her youth and raven beauty,
And in its place, a face carved out by time.

Take care before you're tempted by the moonlight,
And seek the mystery of Mid-summer's eve.
Think twice before your heart becomes enchanted
As through your soul the magic starts to weave.

Beware,
My lovely daughter,
Beware,
How long you stay
Beware,
The Summer Weaver,
For he'll steal your youth away.

Chapter 7

The Festival of Lughnasadh

(Or the Harvest of the First Fruits, or Lammas (Lammastide), originally Anglo Saxon but later incorporated into the Christian calendar.)

Lughnasadh: celebrated Sunset 1st August to Sunset 2nd August. Harvest of the First Fruits, Lammas or Lammastide: celebrated anytime from 1st August dependant upon location, regional customs and the weather.

The festival of Lughnasadh speaks of fullness and bounty of richness and sacrifice. As cornfields ripple in the late summer breeze and whisper golden promises of the grain harvest to come, we know deep within our psyche that the darkness is but a heartbeat away.

On an August evening, when the sun is about to seek new horizons and the full moon hangs heavy in a velvet sky, we become aware of a slight chill, a whisper that the halcyon days are numbered. Daylight lingers a little less and once again we are reminded that the eternal wheel is creaking into the arms of winter.

The Goddess in her pregnancy allows us to gather the first fruits and grain of her harvest, whilst her Lord and consort sacrifices his life and spills his blood upon the fields of corn in order that the earth's continuing cycle of fertility will be assured in the year to come. The face of the Goddess depicts the bountiful mother and yet, here, she turns slightly towards the grieving face of the Crone. She knows, however, that the cycle of life is eternal and that the Lord she now mourns will be reborn from her womb at the Mid Winter solstice.

Carole Carlton

Destiny's Call

I watch you walk in the greenwood,
A portrait of anguish and pain.
I watch you walk in the greenwood,
Knowing you will not walk here again.

Your lady you met in the greenwood,
You married her under the May,
Knowing, deep down, as her consort,
Your life would be asked for one day.

Go swiftly, my Lord, from the greenwood,
Stand tall amid the corn,
For destiny is calling,
As the sun comes up with the dawn.

Die bravely, my Lord of the greenwood,
As the red blood flows from your veins.
Sleep soundly my Lord of the greenwood,
'Til the Oak King rises again.

Festival Origins, History and Myth

As far as the eye could see fields of golden corn rippled and danced in the early August breeze.

'Can you hear it dear?' I jumped at the sound of Mrs Darley's voice just behind me.

'Hear what?' I asked.

'The death-knell of summer,' she replied.

'Oh surely not!' I protested. 'Not just yet, it's only the beginning of August!'

'In a day or two my dear,' said Mrs Darley, 'the golden fields will lie bare and the Corn God will be no more. Listen to the breeze of summer as it rustles gently through the cornfields, for tomorrow it will mourn and carry with it the slight chill of autumn.'

Lughnasadh

The name Lughnasadh (sometimes spelt Lugnasa or Lughnasa and pronounced Loo–nas-ah) is an Irish Gaelic word and, according to some literary sources, means 'The funeral feast of Lugh', whilst others tell us it was simply the Celtic name for the month of August.

Lugh was a Celtic deity, much revered not only in Ireland but also in certain parts of Europe and mainland Britain, with many towns and cities having derived their name from him, including Lyon in France and Carlisle in the north of England.

According to Professor Ronald Hutton, however, Lugh was not a God particularly associated with the corn harvest, and it seems rather strange as to why his name was given to this festival. Nevertheless, Lugh was, a popular God, handsome, heroic and talented. He was an accomplished healer, harpist, poet and magician and is often referred to as 'Lugh the Light Bearer'.

Lammas

The Anglo Saxons also held a celebration at the beginning of August called the 'Hlaefmass' meaning 'Loaf Festival', from where the medieval word 'Lammas' derives. In 921 AD it was recorded that Lammas (also known as the 'Feast of the first fruits') was the festival where the first gathering of grain was made into a loaf which was then consecrated in church, although before Britain was Christianised it was thought that the first gathering of grain was offered up to the Gods as a token of thanks for an abundant harvest.

In medieval Britain, Lammas became an important date upon which fairs were held, rents collected and officials elected, and still today in the South West of England and in Bally Castle, Northern Ireland, Lammas fairs remain important occasions in the community's diary.

Carole Carlton

The Christian period of 'Lammastide' is now often extended up to the end of September or the beginning of October and includes the more familiar 'Harvest Festival', whose origins will be explored in more detail during the following chapter.

Harvesting the corn

In times when the grain was harvested by hand, many traditions and superstitions grew up around this important event.

The cereal harvest was the most labour intensive part of the agricultural year and therefore the reward given for reaping the corn became a very important part of the whole process.

In many cases payment was made in kind, with food and drink being the most popular and this was often provided by the land owners throughout the reaping period. At the end of the corn harvest when all had been safely gathered in, a feast was usually held for all the labourers in final payment for their hard work. This tradition appears to date back to Roman times, where written records tell of grain labourers being rewarded with a feast for their work, obviously the origins of what we now refer to as a 'Harvest Supper'.

In some instances a whole family (with the exception of the mother) would be summoned to complete the harvest and would be rewarded at the end by a gift of bread, milk and meat in payment.

In Cumberland during the seventeenth century, a piper was ordered to play during each day of the harvest, no doubt to help the reaping along. This was probably equivalent to our ipod or radio today!

On rare occasions actual money was paid over to the labourers, but this was not a frequent occurrence. Another popular form of payment was that of alcohol, as was the case on a Devon farm in 1816. It is recorded that late in the afternoon beer or cider was provided along with a large lunch and hearty supper. It is not too hard to appreciate that quite often the labourers would be drunk before the work was completed and in the late 1800s, in the South

East of England, the ration of drink was brought down to seventeen pints per head during the harvest period.

Even up until the mid nineteenth century, many agricultural and harvest customs, which had originated in Greece and ancient Rome, were still being adhered to in many parts of Northern Europe as well as the British Isles including Scotland, Ireland, Wales, Cornwall and certain parts of England, such as Shropshire, Cumbria and Kent.

Sacrificing and Honouring the Last Sheaf

The festival of Lughnasadh, for all its golden glory, carries with it a certain sadness, in that a sacrifice has to be made in order that the fertility of the land will continue in the coming year. As such, the God is called to his destiny and his blood spilt upon the corn for the greater good of the land.

On 2nd August 1100 King William II, known as Rufus because of his red hair, was said to have died in a mysterious hunting accident, although many have speculated that he became the sacrificial victim in a Pagan ritual to ensure that his kingdom would continue to be fertile and prosper.

Many beliefs abound, which hold that the last sheaf of corn was symbolic of the sacrificial God and that held within the grain was a spirit, a fertile life force, making this sheaf one which should be acknowledged and revered at all costs.

In Frazer's book, *The Golden Bough*, this was taken one step further, suggesting that this life force, or spirit, of the corn had a name. In Scotland it was referred to as 'The Maiden' if the corn was cut before Samhain or Halloween, and the 'Cailleach', meaning 'Crone' or 'Old Woman', if it was cut afterwards. The timing of the harvest depended on the location, regional customs and the weather, so could vary by one or two months throughout the country. In Devon and Cornwall the last sheaf was referred to as 'The Neck', a rather more androgynous option, where labourers would call, 'A neck, a neck, a neck, we have a neck', at which point the whole company would cheer.

The farm labourers employed to harvest the corn often displayed a real fear of cutting the last sheaf, due to the fact that they felt they were slaying the spirit of the corn.

Frazer suggested that whoever cut the final sheaf was seen as symbolically taking the life of the Corn Mother or Corn God, which was not considered a particularly auspicious thing to do. It became common practice, therefore, for all the harvesters to gather round the last sheaf of corn and simultaneously hurl their sickles at the sheaf so that no one would know who had killed the spirit of the corn. He tells us: *'...In County Antrim, down to some years ago, when the sickle was finally expelled by the reaping machine, the few stalks of corn left standing last on the field were plaited together; then the reapers, blindfolded, threw their sickles at the plaited corn...'*

Yet paradoxically, although the last sheaf was not an auspicious one to cut, once harvested it was often looked upon as a symbol of success and fruitfulness in the coming year.

Some accounts of the last reaping tell of the labourers standing around the last sheaf, taking it in turns to throw their sickles, and whoever cut it down was allowed to take it home. Here it was dressed and later taken to the harvest supper organised by the farmer or master and would take pride of place at the table, sitting next to the master along with the successful reaper and his wife.

Corn Dollies

Whoever took the final sheaf of corn home would, along with his wife, go about the important practice of 'dressing' it.

Frazer tells us that many simply tied it with a ribbon and after the harvest supper would hang it over their door, to bring good luck to the household. He also mentions that in some traditions the woman who bound the last sheaf would be more than likely to give birth within the year!

In various places throughout Britain and Europe the final sheaf was made into the rough shape of a woman and referred to as either 'the old woman', 'the corn mother', 'the maiden' or 'kern baby', a figure that we are now more likely to refer to as a 'corn dolly', many of which, in more modern times, have become extremely intricate and beautiful. This figure was often decorated with a scarlet ribbon, to represent the blood of the sacrificial corn spirit, and hung over the hearth until the following spring at which point the seeds would be scattered upon the earth at the first planting to ensure fertility for the coming year, hence the corn dolly's association with fecundity.

In later times, farmers made corn dollies for another specific purpose. They would choose four of the longest stalks of wheat and weave them together, beginning just above the ears. When the corn would not bend any further they would twist their woven stems around to make a loop and secure it with ribbon. These loops were called 'favours' and were often worn at the harvest dance pinned to the gentleman's lapel. Apparently the larger the 'Favour', the more 'favourably' he hoped the ladies might look upon him!

Officialdom and settlements

The clement weather at Lughnasadh made August an ideal time for the ancestors to travel around, as muddy tracks became hard and dry, making access to other communities much easier. As a result, this was a time when Justices of the peace would tour the countryside, settling disputes and ordering the payment of debts. Landlords would take the opportunity of collecting their outstanding rents, and local officials became elected.

Apart from official matters, people would often take the opportunity of visiting neighbouring communities for the purposes of feasting, celebrating the harvest, enjoying fairs, horse racing and forging ties, especially those of marriage.

Just as at Beltane, couples could embark on a trial marriage lasting a year and a day, at which point they could decide whether they wanted to continue, or simply walk away. A variation on the Beltane Handfasting Ceremony involved the couple thrusting their hands through a holed stone whilst making their vows.

Carole Carlton

The Sacred Tree of Lughnasadh

The Yew tree has become synonymous with death and is often found in churchyards. The oldest and largest tree is thought to be the Fortingall yew in Scotland, whose girth is said to be 20 metres plus and is estimated to be some 8000 years old. South Hayling in Hampshire can also boast a yew, which is 10 metres in girth and dates back some 3000 years.

The yew is an appropriate choice for this festival, which has death as one of its main themes. The tree, however, also has the miraculous capability of re-birthing itself when, to all intents and purposes, it appears to have died. In this connection it is the perfect tree for Lughnasadh, as the dying God too will be reborn at the winter solstice from the womb of the Goddess.

The outside branches of the tree grow downwards and root themselves back into the earth, from where they form new stems which rise up and around the central trunk, eventually giving the tree a huge girth. The Druids are said to have performed some of their ceremonies under the yew tree and that they viewed the yew as being symbolic of the soul's immortality.

The Irish feel that the yew tree is one of the most ancient living things on earth, and that it was a tree which was brought from 'the other world' at the beginning of time. They acknowledge it as being the most important of the five 'magical trees' (Yew, Oak, Hawthorn, Elder, Rowan).

At all costs, felling should be avoided and in Ross, Scotland, the curse of the yew will befall anyone who attempts to cut it down:

'Well of the yew tree
Well of the yew tree
To thee should honour be given
In hell a bed is ready for him
Who cuts the tree about thine ears.'

In Brittany it was believed that a churchyard yew would spread a root into the mouth of every corpse which entered the graveyard, whilst in Ystradgynlais in Wales, the yew is constantly pruned to ensure it is below belfry level as there is a local belief that if its height exceeds the tower then the end of the world will come!

A Lughnasadh Tale

The preparations for the Lughnasadh celebrations began in earnest at least a week before the event, which was to be held on the first Friday in August.

Both Mrs Darley and Phyllis worked into the small hours for three nights before the festival, baking pasties, scones, savouries and a wonderful 'Lammas Loaf'. The centrepiece of the table, however, was a magnificent salmon (courtesy of Eddie the poacher), decorated with cucumber scales and dressed in dill.

Friends and acquaintances from far and near were invited and it was earmarked as a night to remember, with everyone being asked to bring a bottle of wine and a 'contribution' to share with other guests.

In my restricted thinking at that time, I interpreted 'contribution' to mean 'more drink' and duly arrived with two bottles of Co-op red. I was to learn, however, that the word 'contribution' actually meant something quite different.

Early in the evening Rose, our delightful self-confessed 'earth mother' arrived, complete with her beautifully round belly, adorned with shimmering chiffon and jingling coins, ready to perform her Eastern dance once the wine had begun to flow.

Closely following Rose was Don, another neighbour of some sixty summers, a carpenter and masseur, who brought along a box of homemade herb and cheese straws and a bottle of scented oil, together with a burner with which to fragrance the room.

Midway through the evening a trio of musicians arrived who set up on the pocket of grass outside the cottage door and a mixture of Irish ballads, jigs and reels rang out across the hamlet and beyond.

As dusk was falling, I found myself sitting on the doorstep, listening to the music, when a tanned and tousled young man suddenly appeared at my side.

'You're lonely, yet no-one would ever know,' he said, in a quiet yet matter of fact way, the trace of an Irish lilt vaguely detectable.'

I must have looked somewhat taken aback by these words and he laughed, the sound of which reminded me of a summer waterfall. 'Buy a bunch of lavender and I'll tell your fortune,' he said.

Being somewhat charmed by his rather unorthodox approach, I was just about to explain that I had no money with me when the spell was broken, as Eddie placed his hand on the young man's shoulder and politely asked him to leave.

The young man rose without question and began to walk away along the path, turning as he reached the gate. 'I'll be back to sell you the lavender,' he called.

Turning to Eddie, I said 'Why did you ask him to leave? Who was he?'

'He's just one of the travellers who come down off the high moor, they call round every summer. You couldn't trust them,' he replied, walking away, leaving me feeling a little foolish, yet strangely elated at the thought of the stranger's possible return.

The celebrations continued late into the night, interrupted briefly by a few words from our hostess who, upon ensuring that everyone had a glass in hand, toasted the occasion.

'To the Goddess for her bounty; to her Lord for his sacrifice; and to you all for your generosity; given with love and the essence of your true selves. To Lughnasadh!'

'Lugnasadh!' we cheered.

We sang, we danced, we talked, we laughed, we ate, we drank, but most of all we shared our contributions and I learned, that Lughnasadh night, that true gifts come from the heart and not necessarily from the purse.

MRS DARLEY'S PAGAN WHISPERS

Celebrating Lughnasadh

Lughnasadh is a time for honouring the richness of the earth's bounty and acknowledging the sacrificial element of the season in order to ensure fertility in the coming year.

Making corn dollies under the watchful eye of Mrs Darley was an absolute must for all of us living in the tiny Cornish hamlet on Bodmin Moor. Eddie would gather the corn from a local farmer and soak it overnight, bringing armfuls of it into the summerhouse on the appointed day whilst Phyllis would provide the red ribbon and cord.

Here we would choose our pieces of corn and follow Mrs Darley's instructions on the assembly of the dolly, followed by her firm insistence to remember to scatter the seeds on the earth at the spring equinox to ensure a fertile year.

Mrs Darley, I noticed, always had her corn dolly amidst an arrangement of cornflowers and poppies (albeit they were artificial!). The corn, I was to later understand, represented the God, the red poppies his sacrificial blood and the blue cornflowers his death and this is something I still adhere to today.

One year, courtesy of a local 'crop circle expert', Mrs Darley was invited to Wiltshire to experience first hand what a crop circle in a corn field was like. Upon her return I was eager for her verdict, but to my disappointment and, I suppose, true to form she said little apart from 'Experiential learning is everything my dear, try it sometime!'

Lughnasadh Reflections

This is the time of the earth's corn harvest, when the Goddess gives freely of her first fruits for us to appreciate and enjoy. It should therefore be a time for reflecting upon our own personal harvest of achievement, no matter how large or small.

Look back at the year to date and acknowledge all your successes, give yourself a pat on the back and a treat of some sort whether it's for getting a new job, working through a traumatic event in your life, or caring for the home and family. Every achievement is important and should be acknowledged and celebrated.

Lughnasadh is also a time of sacrifice, albeit thankfully not human in nature, but just as the God gave up his life in order that fertility and growth would be assured for the forthcoming year, perhaps we too should think of things in our lives which no longer serve us or which we have outgrown. It may be as simple as taking a bag of clothes to the charity shop, giving up a destructive habit or as complex as changing jobs or relationships. We all cling to the safe and familiar, but often we have to sacrifice something in order to ultimately enrich our lives.

Lughnasadh Dedication

Find somewhere you will not be disturbed, burn essential oils or incense of your choice and play music if you wish. Take into the room a drink (alcoholic or otherwise), something light to eat, a lighter or matches and one or more candles of yellow or gold to represent the golden cornfields (white will always suffice if you do not have coloured candles).

When you feel ready, dim the lights and light your candle(s).

Now still your mind for a moment or two and become aware of the aroma you have chosen to burn. When you are ready, you may use the dedication below to address the Goddess or, of course, you may wish to write your own. Enjoy this quiet time for as long as you wish and when you have finished, raise a glass to toast the occasion and have something to eat to ground yourself. When you blow out the candles, ask that the energy from the flame be sent somewhere it is needed, rather than direct the energy to yourself.

We all cling to what feels safe and familiar because it is comfortable, because we are frightened to instigate change or simply because we are too lazy to try something new. Occasionally however, we find ourselves being called to jump into the void and to cut the ties that bind, yet ultimately have little

MRS DARLEY'S PAGAN WHISPERS

value. At times such as these, we should perhaps consider making our own personal harvest sacrifice in order that our lives will ultimately become enriched.

<u>Our Lady</u>

Grieving Lady,
Who mourns her Lord within his earthly tomb.

Bountiful Lady,
Whose gifts pour forth from her fertile womb.

Selfless Lady,
Who yields her body to man's greedy hand.

Gracious Lady,
Who breathes life into the heart of this sacred land.

We thank and honour you.

<u>The Lavender Man</u>

Beware, beware the Lavender Man,
The Lavender Man,
The Lavender Man.
Beware, beware the Lavender Man
He'll tempt you with his wares.

Lavender flowers and lavender creams,
Lavender pillows for lavender dreams.

Beware, beware the Lavender Man
He's not all that he seems.

Beware, beware the Lavender Man,

Carole Carlton

The Lavender Man,
The Lavender Man,
Beware, beware the Lavender Man
He'll tempt you with his wares.

Lavender ice and lavender teas,
Lavender honey from lavender bees,

Beware, beware the Lavender Man
He's not all that he seems.

Beware, beware the Lavender Man,
The Lavender Man,
The Lavender Man,
Beware, beware the Lavender Man
He'll lure you to his bed.

Lavender sheets and lavender wine,
Lavender grapes from lavender vines

Beware, beware the Lavender Man
His charms will weave and bind.

Beware, beware the Lavender Man,
The Lavender Man,
The Lavender Man,
Beware, beware the Lavender Man
Were words I did not heed

Beware the man in Lavender guise,
For Lavender lips tell lavender lies.

Beware, beware the Lavender Man
His charms will weave and bind.

Beware, beware the Lavender Man,

MRS DARLEY'S PAGAN WHISPERS

The Lavender Man,
The Lavender Man,
Beware, beware the Lavender Man
He sees into your soul.

For here, beneath the Lavender skies,
Sleeps my child with Lavender eyes.

Beware, beware the Lavender Man…

Chapter 8

The Festival of the Autumnal Equinox

(In close proximity to Michaelmas in the Christian calendar, or the Harvest Festival in the Christian calendar.)

Autumn equinox: Celebrated between the 20th ^{to} 23rd September according to the position of the sun.
Michaelmas: celebrated 29th September.
Harvest Festival: celebrated anytime from 1st August to 31st October according to local customs and traditions, with September being the most popular.

This festival speaks of morning mists, hazy afternoons, and late summer fruits. It is a season of great beauty, where burnished gold meets scarlet red and the earth in her wisdom offers us the last of her summer fruits in exchange for a period of rest and retreat.

This is the second time during the year when day and night are of equal length, but from this day until the winter solstice, daylight hours will decrease as we journey onward into winter.

The Goddess in her dual faced aspect, once again shows us the face of the expectant mother, who offers up the last fruits of her abundant harvest in order that we may be nourished. She also begins to turn a little more towards the face of the crone as she continues to grieve for her sacrificial Lord and breathes a slight autumn chill upon a tired and depleted earth.

The Gathering

The morning breath
Of the autumn serpent

Wraps around the trees
Like a virgin's shroud,
Adorning their fruits
With heavy dew pearls.

Gather, gather the last fruits of summer
Drink of their sweetness
And bathe in their juice,
Gather, gather the last fruits of summer
For winter is binding
And tightening her noose.

The weakening sun
Rising late from its slumber,
Creates a golden haze
Amid the trees,
Calling the last fat fruits
To their destiny.

Gather, gather the last fruits of summer
Drink of their sweetness
And bathe in their juice,
Gather, gather the last fruits of summer
For winter is binding
And tightening her noose.

The winds of change
Rustle through the trees,
As leaves dance free
And fill the air
With scarlet promises,
Whispering of things to come.

Gather, gather the last fruits of summer
Drink of their sweetness
And bathe in their juice,

MRS DARLEY'S PAGAN WHISPERS

Gather, gather the last fruits of summer
For winter is binding
And tightening her noose.

Festival Origins, History and Myth

As I stood on Mrs Darley's doorstep one late September evening, she pointed towards the far horizon of Dartmoor.

'Look at that golden haze settling over the tors.'

'It's lovely,' I agreed.

'Everyone is disappointed when the summer ends,' she mused, 'both seasonally and in life, but the autumn can be quite beautiful, softer somehow and richer in colour.'

'And it gives us an excuse to light our fires,' I smiled.

She nodded, 'Yes, every season has the ability to bring a little warmth into our lives in one way or another.' She disappeared momentarily into the kitchen and returned with a jar of greengage chutney.

'A little something to remind you of summer during the autumn to come,' she smiled. 'Nothing is ever lost as time passes, it merely metamorphoses into something as wonderful or, in some cases, into something even better than before.'

I turned to look at her, somewhat puzzled, but she had already closed the lower part of the stable door and disappeared from view.

The Autumnal Equinox

Once again, as with the spring equinox, much uncertainty abounds regarding this particular festival and its origins and as previously mentioned there is little evidence of the equinoxes being celebrated by our Celtic ancestors, due to the fact that they were more interested in marking the beginning of each season and major agricultural events, rather than the astrological alignment.

The peoples of the Neolithic era, however, appear to have acknowledged the equinoxes in certain parts of the British Isles, as can be evidenced from the passage tombs at Knowth (circa 3200 BC) in County Meath, where one passage is aligned with the equinox sunrise and the other with sunset.

Whatever its history, however, the autumn equinox brings a degree of uniformity to the wheel of the year and is important in its own right on two counts. Firstly, it acts as the mid-point marker of the sun's journey from summer through to winter, and secondly it approximately marks the end of the modern harvest as September is often the preferred time for harvest services and suppers rather than at the festival of Lughnasadh. Whatever its origins and meaning to our ancestors, it is certainly a time worth acknowledgement by modern followers of the seasonal wheel.

As mentioned before, the word 'equinox' simply means 'of equal length' referring to the twelve hours of daylight and twelve hours of darkness. It was originally thought to stem from two Latin words *aequus* meaning equal and *nox* meaning night.

Michaelmas

The word 'Michaelmas' literally means 'the feast of St Michael'. He is the Archangel of the sun and patron Saint of high places, although in the Hebrides he was acknowledged as the Archangel of the sea. Many churches built in elevated positions are dedicated to St Michael.

The Traditional Harvest Festival

Apart from the first sheaf of corn being brought into the church and blessed at Lughnasadh or Lammas in medieval times, little religious importance was given to the gathering of the fruit and vegetable crops, which appears to be for two reasons.

The first being that many of the customs associated with the harvest were seen by the church as being rooted in the Pagan past and, secondly, the gathering of the crops had nothing to do with the actual life of Christ.

In 1843, however, the Reverend Robert Stephen Hawker, the

rather eccentric Vicar of Morwenstow church, which is situated high up on Cornwall's windswept north coast, changed all that and became the first Vicar to openly celebrate a harvest festival in his church.

His community was sparse, poor and often violent, as smuggling and wrecking was a frequent occurrence. It was also one which was steeped in superstition and any customs, which bestowed good luck and fertility, were of great importance to the inhabitants, including those associated with the gathering of the crops.

In the early 1840s, the area suffered from very poor harvests and many parishioners would have gone hungry if their generous Vicar had not been so compassionate. He once wrote: *'If I eat and drink and see my poor people hunger and thirst, I am not a minister of Christ, but a lion that lurketh in his den to ravish the poor.'*

In 1842, however, much to the community's amazement, the harvest was good and special prayers of thanksgiving were ordered by the authorities to be recited in church. Considering this to be a good idea, the following year, on 13th September, the Reverend Hawker issued a summons to the parishioners of Morwenstow to meet him in the chancel of the church on the first Sunday of October for a service of harvest thanksgiving.

The popularity of the service soon began to spread and within twenty years it was in almost every church in the land with appropriate hymns being written such as 'We plough the fields and scatter' and 'Come ye thankful people come'. Churches themselves became lavishly decorated with fruits and vegetables of the season, soon to be accompanied by what has become in many parts the traditional 'Harvest Supper'.

As a writer and poet, Reverend Hawker wrote on several occasions of the Celtic festival of Lughnasadh and is said to have continued the old Saxon custom of making a loaf from the first gathering of corn for use in the Holy Communion Service. He considered the date of the Lughnasadh festival, however, too early for a celebration of all the fruits of the harvest and therefore preferred to wait until late September/early October before holding his service.

Sacred Equinox Plants

At the last gathering of the harvest produce, hops remain both a useful and delightful plant, with rituals that echo those of the corn harvest at Lughnasadh.

In the nineteenth century, at the end of the hop-picking season, a king and queen of the hop field were selected and carried ceremoniously to the farmhouse where they would have the honour of declaring the hop pickers ball and feast open.

Hops of course have been used to flavour beer for centuries, but they also have several other uses. Hanging hops over the beams in a period property is considered today to look attractive and appealing to the eye, but in times gone by hops were hung over the fireplace to ward off evil and ensure good luck for the coming season.

Hops were used to treat certain ailments, and we are told that George III used to take a hop concoction to ease his insomnia. A poultice of hops is said to ease congestion associated with pneumonia, a useful tip to bear in mind as winter approaches.

Fairs and Feasts

As September was and often still is mellow and warm, Michaelmas became a time for fairs, renewing contracts and feasting.

'Mop fairs' were held around this time where servants were formally hired for the year. They stood in a row, each wearing a sign of their trade such as a crook for a shepherd, a pot for a cook, a duster for a maid and so on. Upon hiring them, their employer would give them what was known as a 'fastenpenny', which was money to bind them to their new post at which point they would be allowed to go off around the fair and enjoy themselves.

Horse fairs, sheep fairs and cheese fairs all had their place, but also around this time geese were fattened by allowing them to feed on the stubble of the land following the harvesting of the crops. Their feet were then dipped in tar to make hardened boots in order for them to be marched to market when they would grace the table at the Michaelmas fairs. Both the goose fair in Tavistock and the honey fair in Callington are still held at this time of year in the West Country.

At the village of Abbots Bromley in Staffordshire, on the Monday after the first Sunday after 4th September, one of the oldest customs in Britain is still practiced after some 1000 years. Six men carry reindeer antlers on their shoulders accompanied by a Maid Marian (who is a man dressed as a woman, a figure suggested by Colin and Janet Bord as someone who represents polarity in being both male and female), a fool, a hobby-horse and a boy with a bow and arrow. Its origins are shrouded in mystery, but suggestions include that it was originally performed as a ritual to ensure good deer hunting, that it was a dance to honour the sacrificial God, or simply a celebration of the fruits of the earth and meant to bestow luck, health and success upon all those who watched (and still watch) it.

In Scotland on the eve of Michaelmas, wild birdseed would be scattered outside the home in order that the feeding birds would bring good luck to the household during the coming winter, whilst on Michaelmas Day itself a St Michael's cake was made of grain from every crop grown in the fields that year and served with lamb.

An Autumn Equinox Tale

It was around 6pm when I finally drove up the lane into the last vestiges of Cornish sunshine, which did much to lift my spirits after a week spent on a course in Bristol.

As I approached the cottage, I was amazed to see an array of cars parked everywhere and, upon making my way through the five-barred gate, I became aware of laughter and a voice emanating from Mrs Darley's garden.

'But no, this cannot be, I will search the land for my beloved daughter and will not rest until I find her...'

The voice was unmistakably that of Mrs Darley and, intrigued, I peered over the garden gate, to become witness to the most delightful of scenes.

An array of people sitting on various stools and chairs arranged in a somewhat higgledy-piggledy fashion were visible at the top of the garden, whilst at the bottom, against the backdrop of Dartmoor, stood (I was later to learn) the 'cast' of 'Demeter and Persephone', including of course the inimitable Mrs Darley as Demeter, Lucy (Rose's teenage daughter) as Persephone, Dan was the white bearded Zeus and Bod appeared as a most foreboding Hades, Lord of the Underworld.

In a short moment of 'exit stage left' for Mrs Darley, she noticed me hanging over the gate and beckoned me enter. I sank down on the grass beside Phyllis' chair. She smiled as she patted me on the shoulder and whispered, 'A short bout of Harvest madness...it's Demeter and Persephone, all in a good cause though.'

I nodded as Mrs 'Demeter' Darley returned to the stage and proceeded to give Zeus what can only be described as a 'proper roasting', upon his refusal to tell her the whereabouts of her beloved daughter, Persephone. At once Demeter, the beautiful Greek Corn Goddess, threatened to withdraw her hand from the earth, which Zeus knew would result in the land lapsing into eternal winter, unless Persephone was returned to her. Zeus began to panic, knowing Demeter to be a woman of her word and eventually disclosed that Persephone was currently residing in the underworld, having been captured by the Dark Lord, Hades. He deemed that Persephone should be returned to Demeter, on condition that she had not eaten whilst in the underworld. Sadly for Demeter, her daughter had partaken of four seeds from the fruit of the pomegranate whilst under the care of Hades and, as such, was destined to spend four months in the underworld with him and return to the earth for the remaining eight months to be in the company of her mother, whose joy would be expressed by the return of the light and the fertility of the land.

To rapturous applause the play ended and what can only be described as a sumptuous feast followed, with all the wholesome ingredients that harvest tide brings.

'Hello dear', said Mrs Darley, who greeted me with a warm hug. 'Do join in, there's plenty of everything to go round.'

'I feel so guilty though…I haven't brought anything…I didn't realise…' I began.

'Well of course you didn't. If it makes you feel any better we've charged everyone £2.50 for the play and the money is going to buy food hampers for the elderly of the area at Yule, so if you want to contribute please do, Phyllis is collecting the money. This, my dear,' she explained 'is our harvest and equinox festival combined. It's all based on a celebration of food to acknowledge the abundance of the earth, so that we may feast together as friends and that we may also share the earth's bounty with those who are perhaps less fortunate than ourselves. From now on Demeter will withdraw her hand from the earth and we will turn towards winter until Persephone is returned to her at Imbolc.'

'What a delightful take on the reason why we descend into our miserable winter,' I mused.

'Winter is only miserable dear, if that is your perception. Change your perception and winter can be one of the most beautiful of seasons. Yes the trees are bare, yes the days are short, yes the sun is weak, but from the cold barren earth life will emerge and both Persephone's sojourn to the Underworld and Demeter's subsequent mourning will not be in vain, for love is eternal and can survive any parting.'

She turned and walked away to speak to others who demanded her attention and, as I watched the sun disappear over the back of Sharp Tor, I inwardly welcomed the season that was to come.

Celebrating the Autumn Equinox

This is a time for enjoying the last fruits, and preserving and preparing for the onset of winter.

In honour of this, Mrs Darley would invite the children of the hamlet along with as many adults as wished to accompany them to go on a treasure hunt with a list of items to collect. These included collecting blackberries, apples, damsons, plums and conkers. The children were always told to look out for a blackberry arch as this is said to confer healing, especially if it is crawled through from east to west on a sunny day and is said to be most beneficial in cases of boils, rheumatism and blackheads!

Upon our return we would all pile into Mrs Darley's cottage, which was always decorated in golds and oranges, reds and browns in order to reflect the new season, and once inside we were greeted with the irresistible smell of warm herb bread and spiced tea.

Following these wonderful autumn treats the children would hand out a conker (if they had managed to find any!) to all those present, to confer success as well as easing ailments such as chills, rheumatism and backache. A strict warning was always given, however, never to eat them as they are poisonous.

During this time of welcoming in the autumn season, Mrs Darley and Phyllis would make bottles of preserves and sell them at their autumn play in order to raise money for the elderly at Christmas, whilst the collectors of the fruit were all treated to a fruit pie, as a token of thanks for their work.

Autumn Equinox Reflections

Our second equinox of the year once again calls us to review our lives and restore balance. For now the hours of light and dark are equal and the fierce heat of the summer gives way to the mellow warmth of autumn. It is a time to curb excesses, to complete tasks and move calmly into a quieter time of year.

It is a time for prevention and preparation, for putting things in place before the onset of winter. This could be as simple as re-organising finances in readiness for the Yuletide celebrations, or ensuring that Granny has her rotten front door replaced before the weather changes. It is also a time for building up our own personal reserves and looking to review our diet or taking supplements to strengthen our immune system before the season of coughs and colds begins.

Just as at the spring equinox, this festival provides us with an excellent opportunity to clear out clutter, especially in the store cupboard. Throw out all those old packets, jars and tins which have long passed their sell by date and make room for healthy pulses, nuts and pickles from this year's harvest.

If you are interested in more national or global issues, then it may be an appropriate moment to think about either giving time to a charity to ensure that the vulnerable can be helped through the coming winter or, if time is not an option, then a donation would also be very welcome.

Although many people see the dark evenings as something to dread and fear, the darkness should be seen as a gift. Use the evenings to undertake a new interest or qualification at night class and an opportunity to meet like-minded people as the new academic year begins. Alternatively, use a few evenings a week to catch up on some reading, practise meditation or simply sit and chat over a meal with the family, a friend or partner without the aid of televisions, DVDs or computers.

Although the Goddess begins to turn her face toward the crone, it is time to remember that the autumn is rich in colour and rich in wisdom, just as we become in the autumn of our lives. Do not dismiss it, use its gifts, delight in its grandeur and enjoy!

Harvest Dedication

Find somewhere you will not be disturbed, burn essential oils or incense of your choice and play music if you wish. Take into the room a drink (alcoholic or otherwise), something light to eat, a lighter or matches and one or more candles of red, orange or gold to represent autumnal leaves (white will always suffice if you do not have coloured candles).

When you feel ready, dim the lights and light your candle(s).

Carole Carlton

Now still your mind for a moment or two and become aware of the aroma you have chosen to burn. When you are ready, you may use the dedication below to address the Goddess or, of course, you may wish to write your own. Enjoy this quiet time for as long as you wish and, when you have finished, raise a glass to toast the occasion and have something to eat to ground yourself. When you blow out the candles, ask that the energy from the flame be sent somewhere it is needed rather than direct its path yourself.

The Last Fruits

Lady of the final harvest
Who teaches me:

Preparation,
Preservation,
Contemplation.

Lady of the last fruits
I honour your bounty.

The Circle

Her grief is tangible,
Pouring out upon the sacred land
Which melts
Beneath her burning tears.

The coiling serpent of pain
Twists around her soul,
Injecting despair and desolation.

His touch, she remembers
Through the soft kiss of the wind,

MRS DARLEY'S PAGAN WHISPERS

And silently she yearns.

The Whispering Knights,
Guardians of ancient secrets,
Offer solace.
She closes her eyes
And lays bare her heart.

All at once,
Entranced,
Her tearful soul
Moves within an ancient landscape,
Where all is strange,
And yet...

Within the circle,
Ablaze with flame,
She sees him.

With chalice raised,
He hails the ripened moon,
Turning,
He meets her gaze.
'Thou art Goddess' He whispers.

She smiles
Through the illusion of time.
For love is eternal.

Chapter 9

The Festival of Samhain

(Also known as Halloween, or The Festival of the Dead, 'All Saints' and 'All Souls' in the Christian calendar.)

Samhain: celebrated Sunset 31st October to Sunset 1st November.
Halloween: celebrated 31st October.
All Saints: celebrated 1st November.
All Souls or the Festival of the Dead: celebrated 2nd November.

The festival Of Samhain speaks of rest and retreat, reflection and solitude. It is a time when the last few leaves desert the naked trees and the earth becomes dark and still.

Today this festival honours the dead and the shadow side of our nature. It is a time to go within to acknowledge all aspects of our true selves and to offer a word of gratitude to everyone and everything that has gone before and helped make us what and who we are. It is a time to be welcomed rather than feared and to understand that death is part of the sacred whole. For without knowledge of the darkness we cannot appreciate the light and, from a resting and barren earth, life will once again spring forth.

Although still depicting a duel aspect at Samhain, the pregnant Goddess now turns her face to show the imposing dark mother, wise crone or hag, who has withdrawn her hand from the earth in order to allow decay, death and eventual rebirth to take place.

The God, meanwhile, remains as a shadowy figure awaiting his rebirth at the next festival.

The Dark Realms

Through the mists of other worlds,

Through the veil between,
Come to me in dream and trance,
Come by means unseen.

Lead me through the barren land
Where leaves and needles fall,
Lead me to the darkened heath
Where ghosts and demons call.

Take me to the world beyond,
A world of stick and bone,
Take me to the shadow realms,
The dwelling of the crone.

Let me see the well of death,
The cauldron of decay,
Let me come to know the hag
Once crowned the 'Queen of May'.

Wisest Hecate, dark Cailleach,
Who bring us loss and pain
Lead us through the door of death,
That we may rise again.

Festival Origins, History and Myth

Returning home early one afternoon in late October, I was accosted by Mrs Darley who was, she informed me, just about to go for a walk down the little copse adjacent to the cottages. She asked me to join her and, although I had work to do, I knew the walk would turn out to be far more rewarding than sitting at my lap top.

I quickly changed into something more practical for walking and was soon plunging down into the little copse amid the decaying and blackened leaves.

'Ah,' she said, pointing at the ground. 'Mushrooms! The earth is beginning her season of rest, and these beautiful fungi rise through the forest floor as they heed the wishes of the Goddess and begin the task of clearing away decaying and rotting vegetation.'

'Do they really?' I asked, peering at a particularly plump brown specimen with a spongy lemon underside.

'That's a boletus,' Mrs Darley informed me. 'It's a fascinating subject, fungi, if you take the time to read up on it. Without them the woods would be overrun with decomposing matter.' She paused and her voice lowered as if imparting a secret, 'It is of course the time of the dark Goddess, she who brings death and decay.'

I shivered and suddenly became aware of the rapidly fading light as the setting sun ushered in a misty moon, and I thought longingly of the cosy fire in Mrs Darley's hearth.

'Never fear death, my dear,' she said, touching my arm as she noticed my alarmed expression. 'How can we fear the Goddess as the bringer of death when it is also she who offers us life and rebirth?'

I smiled, 'Like a circle?'

'Like a circle,' she said.

Samhain

The name Samhain (pronounced Sow-een) is an Irish Gaelic word and literally means 'summer's end'. The ancient Celts only recognised two seasons, those of winter and summer. The festival of Beltane celebrated the entrance of summer, whilst Samhain heralded the beginning of winter and was recognised as the most important festival of the year. According to Irish and Welsh folklore, the evening of Samhain was the Celtic equivalent to our New Years Eve, or 'Old year's night' as it is known in Ireland, although there is no firm literary evidence for this.

It was a time when Kings would gather their tribes, and we are informed from twelfth century writings that the celebrations and feasting lasted for three days before Samhain and three days after it.

Irish settlers who went to Scotland took the name of Samhain with them, but to the Welsh, this festival was known as 'Calan Gaeaf', meaning 'the first day of winter', or 'Nos Galan Aea' meaning 'winter's eve'.

Although in the main Samhain primarily marked the end of the old year, the beginning of winter and the time when the cattle were brought in from pasture, we are led to believe that the North European Celts also honoured their dead at this festival, a ritual which is thought to date back to between 1000 BC and 10 BC.

Time to say 'Goodbye'

As the festival of Samhain marked the onset of winter, it was very much a time for saying goodbye on many levels.

Animals were brought in from their summer pasture and decisions had to be made about which livestock, should be kept and which should be slaughtered, in order to see the community through a harsh winter.

It was also a time when families understood that frail members of the community would probably not be strong enough to survive the harsh winter which lay ahead. Naturally they found this sad, and grieved as we would, but they did have a much healthier understanding of life and death than perhaps we do today and accepted that death was a natural part of the continuing cycle of life.

Samhain heralded a time when travel between neighbouring tribes was put on hold until at least the spring, as well worn tracks would become muddy and therefore impossible to negotiate. Communities, therefore, kept very much to themselves during the dark time ahead.

Parting the veil between this world and the next

To the Celts, Samhain was a time when the normal laws were suspended and was one of three times during the year when the veil between the worlds was at its thinnest. It was accepted that upon this night the spirits of the dead could return and roam the earth, and it therefore became customary to leave offerings of food outside the door for them, in the hope that they would stay outside and not venture into the home.

If the food was gone in the morning, it was taken that the spirits had accepted it, which was considered to be an auspicious sign for the household concerned. No one who had an ounce of common sense would steal food left out for the dead, except perhaps the homeless who probably found this a most fortunate time of year!

As darkness closed in and people sat around the fire it became traditional to tell ghostly tales, whilst those who had the gift of 'sight' would predict the future in the flames of the fire. It became a time for acknowledging that there were other worlds of existence besides the earthly plane and, in Ireland, bonfires are still lit on Halloween to celebrate this ancient festival.

The realm of the fairy was also believed to be open to mere mortals, and in Ireland it was believed that at Samhain the fairies would often let humans catch a glimpse of their world, sometimes playing haunting music with which to bewitch them and make them want to dance. If the fairies succeeded in keeping them entertained until dawn, then the veil would fall and they would be trapped in the fairy kingdom for a year, until the veil once again lifted.

At that time the mortal would be given free choice as to whether they wished to return or stay in the fairy realms. Very occasionally humans have taken the decision to return, but allegedly none have lived very long afterwards to tell the tale!

A time of fire and sacrifice

It was thought that the Gods drew near to the earth at Samhain, and in parts of Ireland and Scotland it became a time of sacrifice by fire, both to appease the Gods and to ensure that the tribe would have a safe progression through the night of Samhain and the dark days of the coming winter. In some traditions a poor vagabond would be called upon to give up his life, whilst in others an elderly King from one of the tribes would be the sacrificial victim.

It has been suggested that Bonfire night on 5th November became the new Samhain and that the church latched onto the idea of Guy Fawkes, who attempted to blow up the houses of parliament, in order to Christianise the original Celtic festival.

This, however, was not the case, as in England Samhain was seldom celebrated and the commemoration of the foiling of the Gun powder plot was a decision taken by parliament in 1606 to mark the safe passage of the houses of parliament through the events of 5th November 1605. It was declared that everyone should attend a church service on the morning of 5th November to give thanks for the prohibition of this crime. It became so popular in Protestant England that by 1625 great bonfires were being held and effigies of Guy Fawkes were being burned. Strangely, however, Guy Fawkes was actually sentenced to be hung, drawn and quartered rather than burned, although he did manage to escape this horrific end by launching himself from the high scaffold and broke his neck before the crown could have its revenge.

Protection rites

Bonfires were only one aspect of protection during this dangerous night. In Celtic times, the Irish often favoured the use of a 'Parshell' hung over their door, which was a rough cross of sticks woven with rushes, whilst others included the use of salt and iron to protect their homes. In the far Scottish Isles, burning lumps of peat were carried around the perimeters of the home in order to provide protection to the inhabitants. Other rituals included placing salt in the keyholes to prevent witches from entering and killing a cockerel in order to nail its tail feathers over the stable door to protect the cattle.

MRS DARLEY'S PAGAN WHISPERS

Trick or Treat and 'Jack o'lanterns'

Trick and treating has its origins in the old Celtic beliefs of leaving out offerings for the visiting dead on Samhain. Eventually people began to dress up as 'Guisers' (disguising themselves) to imitate the departed souls, and demanded food or drink from neighbours to prevent them from playing tricks on their homes or cattle. In the eighteenth century it was recorded that youths banged on doors, turned cattle around in their byres and stole cabbages and, not surprisingly, in some parts of Ireland this became known as 'Mischief Night'.

These customs eventually travelled across the Atlantic with the Irish during the 1800s and were immediately embraced by the Americans, where they were elaborated upon and returned to Britain with both American and Irish immigrants during the nineteenth century. Upon their return, more daring tricks were recorded including the lighting of cabbage stalks and the resulting smoke blown through key holes, chimneys being blocked and horses being released from their stables, with treats taking the form of money or sweets. 'Guising' also returned and now Halloween costumes are as diverse as ghosts, ghouls, skeletons, monsters and witches.

Lighted lanterns with carved faces were made from turnips and mangles, known as 'Spunkies' or 'Punkies' in the West Country or 'Jack o'lanterns' in Eastern England, these being terms given to the mysterious lights produced by gases released from the marshes. These lighted lanterns were carried around the village in the hope that they would scare the unpopular people of the village, although many people hung them outside to scare away unwanted spirits. With the American immigrant influence, turnips gave way to pumpkins which were easier to carve.

The Sacred Tree of Samhain

The sacred tree of Samhain is the apple tree, and although at Samhain the tree stands gnarled and bare, the fruits of the tree will have been safely gathered in, in readiness for their role in the Samhain celebrations.

The apple tree was always thought to belong to the Goddess and represented a gaining of knowledge and wisdom (hence its important role in the temptation of Adam by Eve in the Garden of Eden). It was seen as a tree of protection and one which awakened insight. Indeed, when an apple is sliced horizontally a five pointed star can be seen which has, over millennia, become a sign of sacred wisdom and power.

It was thought that the apple tree grew at the heart of the Celtic 'Otherworld', or 'Avalon', and had magical properties. Many sailors were said to have crossed the Western Seas to find this mysterious land, and the traditional game of 'Apple Bobbing' has its origins in this old tale as being symbolic of the sailors bobbing on the sea. Folklore tells us that anyone successful in retrieving an apple whilst 'bobbing' will be sure to live through another year, whilst if the 'bobbed' apple is eaten then eternal youth will also be bestowed!

Apples also meant fertility and thirteen apples (one for every moon of the year) were buried after the final harvest to ensure that next year's harvest would be good.

An old custom for girls who wished to know the initial of the man they would marry also involved an apple. They would peel an apple and then wait until the stroke of midnight at which point they would throw the peel over their shoulder and the letter, which formed, would provide a clue as to the initial of their future husband.

Halloween and All Saints

The more familiar name of Halloween actually derives from the Christianised 'Festival of Saints', originally called 'Hallowtide', 'Hollentide', 'Allantide', 'All Hallows' or 'All Saints', celebrated these days on 1st November. The word 'Halloween' literally means 'Eve of Hallowtide' and is now celebrated on the evening of 31st October.

MRS DARLEY'S PAGAN WHISPERS

It is thought that 'Hallow' itself comes from either the Saxon word 'halig', meaning 'holy', or a medieval English word, 'haelou', meaning Saint.

All Saints day is often thought to be the Christianised version of the Celtic festival of Samhain, but back in the fourth century it was held in the Mediterranean area of Europe during the month of May and was in respect of everyone martyred under the Pagan Emperors of Rome. During the fifth century the date moved to Easter, then to Pentecost and finally in the ninth century the churches of England and Germany began to celebrate it on 1st November, although the Irish Christians continued to resist this change for as long as possible, preferring to use their original date of 20th April.

All Souls and The Festival of the Dead

At the end of the tenth century a new festival came into being, that of 'All Souls'. The Abbot of Cluny ordered a mass for the Christian dead in his own and all associated monasteries, which he originally held in February. So popular was this new idea that many Catholic churches adopted the same festival, which gradually began to incorporate all departed souls and became known as either 'The Festival of the Dead' or 'All Souls'. Eventually it was agreed that it should be moved to 2nd November to make a three-day festival to include 'All Hallows Eve' on 31st October, 'All Saints' on the 1st November and 'All Souls' on 2nd November.

This is a wonderful time to visit ancient burial mounds, quoits, dolmen tumuli, barrows or even the local grave yard in order that those who have gone before are honoured or remembered. Recommended sites include West Kennet Long Barrow close to Avebury in Wiltshire, Newgrange just outside Dublin or Trevethy Quoit just on the edge of Bodmin Moor in Cornwall.

In Antrobus in Cheshire, at the beginning of November, a 'Soul-cakers' play (similar to a mummers play of old) is performed in the pubs over a two-week period. Characters include a 'wild horse', King George, The Black Prince, The 'Quack' Doctor, Mary (a 'she' male) and Beelzebub.

A Samhain Tale

The scattering of Tommy's ashes was a strange affair and had, as its centre piece, a Rowan tree planted as a token of thanks upon the birth of Mrs Darley's grandson.

Tommy was Mrs Darley's brother-in-law, a frequent visitor to the cottage for all matters of D.I.Y. His death was quite unexpected and, following his cremation in London, his ashes were brought back to Cornwall by Mrs Darley for scattering in the garden he helped to tend.

'We're casting Tommy to the four quarters, dear, on Wednesday morning at 11.15, most appropriate as it's just a few moments before the rising of the new moon and also happens to be 'The Festival of Dead', otherwise known as Samhain,' she said, obviously hoping that would make everything so much clearer for me. 'It's in the garden. Can you be there?'

I heard myself making excuses about work and meetings as I felt this was an occasion to avoid at all costs, but as the week wore on I became increasingly curious and finally decided to take the morning off to attend this rather strange ceremony.

As the due time approached the weather turned cold, cloudy and typically autumnal in nature. I waited until I saw other people arriving and, wrapping up warmly, went to join them in Mrs Darley's garden.

'Ah yes, over here dear, we need a woman in the east,' she said, manoeuvring me around one side of the tree.

Once in position, I had time to acknowledge my three fellow guests who included Phyllis, Eddie the poacher, Peter and, of course, Tommy, who was carefully contained within a black casket.

At 11.15am Mrs Darley raised her arms to the darkening sky and began to walk clockwise around the tree calling the four quarters, and bidding us join hands to form a circle. She then called upon the Dark Moon Goddess, Hekate, to take Tommy's earthly remains to rest in the arms of the dark mother. She proceeded to remove the lid from the casket and, much to my horror, bid us each take a handful of ashes and cast them to the elements and direction in which we were standing.

My words were carefully typed on a slip of paper, and I read aloud, 'To the elements of air and the keepers of the eastern winds may Tommy's remains rest in the arms of the Dark Mother'.

Similar phrases were spoken by the other quarters, using the elements of fire, water and earth, with the final words being spoken by Mrs Darley, as she cast the remaining ashes to the wind.

'With many blessings, may Tommy's soul rise on the wings of the Maiden moon Goddess Selene.'

We all stood in silence. The late October wind was attempting to bite its way through us, yet no one felt the cold, only the warmth created by this unusual yet strangely moving ceremony.

Celebrating Samhain

In keeping with the traditions of Samhain being both a time of introspection and feasting, Mrs Darley always held a two-part celebration, which was always a firm favourite with everyone in the hamlet.

The festivities would begin as soon as the children arrived home from school or earlier if Samhain fell at the weekend. Mrs Darley would have a variety of beautiful cards, glitter and paints available with which to make masks for the evening celebrations, and the adults would need little encouragement to make one for themselves, after which several pumpkins would be carved out and candles placed in each. With this accomplished the children were sent home whilst the food was attended to and to get ready for the real Samhain evening ahead.

None of us were permitted to go round to Mrs Darley's cottage until the children, dressed in their ghoulish outfits, had visited every cottage in the hamlet to trick or treat. By 7.00pm we would all squeeze into Mrs Darley's cottage, which was a vision of purple and yellow in order to symbolise the ending of the old Celtic year and the beginning of the new, and then the festivities would begin in earnest with apple bobbing, chestnuts roasting on the open fire and, of course, the telling of ghost stories.

With the children tired and ready for bed by ten, the evening would have a change of mood and Mrs Darley would usually invite Mia, a dark mysterious lady from the village at the bottom of the moor, to divine or read for those who wished to know a little about their future. Following this we would sit in silence to remember those who had gone before, and join Mrs Darley in a toast to the dark Goddess and the beginning of the new Celtic season of winter.

We were all encouraged to place a morsel of food from the table on an old enamel plate outside the door in order that any visiting ancestors could refresh themselves.

Samhain Reflections

Due to a culmination of Celtic, Christian and more modern influences, Samhain has become a time when the dead are remembered and 'Trick and Treating' has become a well-established tradition, whilst for our Celtic ancestors it was a time of preparation and protection to carry them through the dark times ahead. In our modern society, we too can incorporate both the ancient and modern aspects of Samhain into our personal celebrations.

Use the time to honour and send loving thoughts to those who have gone before, perhaps bringing out old photographs or re-reading letters from family and friends who have moved beyond the veil.

Enjoy the season by throwing a party for children and adults alike, playing games, 'trick or treating' and dressing up, just as the 'Guisers' did in times gone by.

Use the increasing darkness as a time to retreat and reflect, to turn the attention inward, to look at where and who we are and to remember and acknowledge people and events that have brought us to this moment. This is quite a difficult process to undertake, as often it is far easier to look at everyone else's lives and problems rather than our own and it is a task which often proves to be quite painful.

We all have a shadow side, a side which we often choose to ignore or deny, especially to others. This is the part of us which is full of fears, dark thoughts and insecurities. However, if we do not face this shadow part of ourselves and acknowledge and appreciate all aspects of who we really are, then it becomes increasingly difficult to live a life full of joy and love.

We must also consider the face of the Goddess as not only the expectant mother, but also that of the wise crone and appreciate that age brings its own treasures, which are not always apparent to a modern society where youth is God.

In age there is wisdom, in age there is knowing, in age there is understanding, in age there is patience. In age lies an inner beauty, which cannot be bought or manufactured, but can only be gained through living and experiencing.

All of us can appreciate the beauty and wisdom of the crone, regardless of our age or sex. If you are dancing in the dawn of youth, or bathing in the wonderment of motherhood, give a thought to those around you who hold the life experiences of the crone. Part their aging veil and look beyond the greying hair and wrinkled faces, drink deeply from their well of knowledge and appreciate their life experiences, for youth is fleeting and the crone beckons us all.

If you are entering, or have entered, the realm of the crone be joyful, for this is a time of liberation, where worries of an external nature can be put aside in favour of inward contemplation and spiritual enlightenment. The confidence and experience of a life fully lived can be its own attractor and earthly pleasures are still there not only to be enjoyed but also celebrated.

Samhain may not be the time for action, but it is a time for acknowledging the needs of the sub-conscious, our true inner selves, and perhaps for the first time to discover and appreciate who we really are.

Samhain Dedication

Find somewhere you will not be disturbed, burn essential oils or incense of your choice and play music if you wish. Take into the room a drink (alcoholic or otherwise), something light to eat, a lighter, matches and one or more candles, either of purple or black to represent the Dark Mother and the resting earth (white will always suffice if you do not have coloured candles).

When you feel ready, dim the lights and light your candle(s).

Now still your mind for a moment or two and become aware of the aroma you have chosen to burn. When you are ready you may use the dedication below to address the Goddess, or of course you may wish to write your own. Enjoy this quiet time for as long as you wish and, when you have finished, raise a glass to toast the occasion and have something to eat to ground yourself. When you blow out the candle ask that the energy from the flame is sent somewhere it is needed, rather than direct the energy yourself.

Eternity

Every moment a new breath,
Every breath a new beginning.

Goddess of expectation
Goddess of transformation
Goddess of regeneration

Every moment a new death,
Every death a new beginning.

The Mermaid

Intermittent moonlight

MRS DARLEY'S PAGAN WHISPERS

Silvers her greying hair
And I become aware
That the woman I live with is ageing.

Upon a once perfect canvas,
Lines are worn,
Where time has drawn
Its hand across her face.

I yearn for youth and beauty,
One to excite
And bring delight,
To satisfy my longing.

Restless like the windswept night,
I leave our bed,
Not one word said
And wander down to the sea.

Every sense is heightened
As wild and free,
The roar of the sea
Thunders onto an empty shore.

Amid white horses
I watch her ride,
On the rising tide
Toward me.

Just out of reach,
Her sea green eyes
They hypnotise
And bewitch my soul.

Upon the breath of the wind
She sings to me,

Carole Carlton

Across the sea
With a voice of woven silver.

'Do not seek what cannot be,
For dreams of lust
Will turn to dust
And die upon the sand.

In the marriage bed
Your Goddess lies,
Her youthful eyes
Still shine behind an ageing veil.

Part the veil and there beyond,
Your mermaid fair,
With silver hair
Will rise and meet your longing.'

Chapter 10

The Winter Solstice

(Also known as Yuletide, or Christmas in the Christian calendar.)

The winter solstice celebrated according to astrological alignment, between 20th to 23rd December. The festive period, however, continues to 5th January to include the Festival of Twelfth Night.

Christmas or Yuletide celebrated 25 December until 6th January to include the twelve days of Christmas and the Epiphany.

The festival of the winter solstice speaks of darkness and light, of endings and beginnings. Yet, from the darkest abyss shines the greatest light and amid the short frosted days of December our sun is reborn. This is a festival of joy and thanksgiving, to celebrate the return to the light at the beginning of a new solar year.

Now we see the Goddess in her triple aspect. She is the crone or wise woman, who has withdrawn her hand from the earth and carries us with her to the darkest point of the year. She is the mother, giving birth to her son/lover and brings us joyous tidings that the sun will once again begin to warm the earth. She is also the maiden, who waits in the wings in readiness to return to the earth at the festival of Imbolc.

The God is born to his expectant Mother and for the moment lies safe within her arms, blissfully unaware that the Sisters of Fate, or Moirai, are already standing in the shadows in readiness to spin, weave and ultimately cut his fragile thread of life.

The Birth

Beneath the sacred oak
Where the cold earth yields to slumber
And the only heartbeat
Is the sole call of the wild,
There lies a darkened hollow
Where our mother lies in waiting,
Waiting for her labour
To bring forth the solstice child.

Rise sweet child of winter,
Rise sweet child of Yule,
Rise again our Oaken King
The Lord of all misrule.

Festival Origins, History and Myth

Leaving for work one morning just as it was getting light, a few days before Christmas, I could just make out the silhouette of Mrs Darley sitting on her doorstep, wrapped cosily in a warm shawl. Thinking she was locked out, I asked if she needed any help.

She shook her head, 'No thank you dear, I'm waiting.'

'I see,' I said, not wishing to ask for whom.

'I'm waiting for the sun,' she said, answering my silent question. 'This is one of the most momentous occasions of the northern hemisphere when the sun begins his journey back to full strength. Most people let it slip by without a word, without even knowing. You should stay a moment.'

'I can't,' I said, 'I have an early meeting.'

'So have I,' said Mrs Darley, her eyes never wavering from the distant horizon.

Solstice

The word 'solstice' is a Latin word which simply means 'the

standing still of the sun', and at both this and the summer solstice, the sun stands still for a few days before (in this case) the increase in light becomes noticeable.

It is difficult to be precise as to whether the Celtic peoples of these islands actually celebrated the winter solstice as such, although we do know that it was probably an important time for their ancestors.

The inhabitants of the Boyne Valley in County Meath marked the importance of this solar event as far back as 3200 BC, before the time of both the pyramids and Stonehenge. This theory is evidenced by the construction of an imposing passage grave, known as 'Brugh na Boinne' or Newgrange.

For approximately five days around the time of the winter solstice, the rising sun shines through a roof box positioned above the entrance to the tomb and penetrates the depths of the triple chambered tomb at dawn.

It is estimated that the tomb took at least 40 years to build and is, no doubt, an indication as to how important the deceased ancestors were to the Neolithic peoples of Ireland, due to the precision and care that was taken in aligning the passage and burial chambers with the solstice sunrise.

It is well worth a visit, but it is worth noting however that out of 25,000 people who put their names down to enter the tomb in December 2004, only 50 were successful, as space is limited. If you choose to visit at a different time of year, the guide will let you experience the effect of the winter solstice sunrise, albeit with the help of an electric light bulb.

An alternative suggestion may be to try the burial chamber at Stoney Littleton near Radstock in the Cotswolds, which is also a passage tomb illuminated by the winter solstice sunrise.

Roman influences

We are aware that the Romans celebrated in grand style at this, the darkest time of year, although it has to be said that the Romans were not sure as to the exact date of the winter solstice.

The Roman writer Pliny took a guess at 26th December, Columella suggested the 23rd, whilst Julius Caesar plumped for 25th December in his official calendar. All these guesses were understandable, for it must have been difficult to be exact without the aid of science and the knowledge that the actual solstice differs each year according to astrological alignment.

The Romans, however, held two distinct festivals at this time of year. The first marked the beginning of the festive season and was called 'Saturnalia', or 'The feast of Saturn', whilst the second marked the end of the season and the beginning of the Roman New Year and was called 'The Kalendae' (the origin of our word 'calendar') and was sacred to the Roman God Janus (the origin of the word January).

The religious part of the festival of Saturnalia was confined to 17th December, but the celebrations continued from between two and seven days afterwards. During this time shops, schools and courts were closed, gambling was allowed in the public domain and presents of candles were exchanged as symbols of light. Groups of male friends would draw lots to see who would be crowned 'King' and this person would then be in control of party games, often wild in nature, definitely a time of 'Misrule'!

The festival of Kalendae was celebrated between 1st and 3rd January where gifts of sweet foods or coins were exchanged to bring luck throughout the coming year.

In the third century AD, the Emperor Aurelian established a new festival, which fell between the Saturnalian and Kalendae celebrations. The date chosen for this festival was 25th December and was called 'Sol Invictus' or 'The invincible sun'.

Christian Influences

With the arrival of Christianity, the celebration of Christ's birth eventually became fixed during the fourth century as 25th December, evidenced in the calendar of Philocalus in 354 CE. This was of course the date of Julius Caesar's official marking of the winter solstice (although mistakenly) and Aurelian's festival of Sol Invictus. Using this date meant that the transition from the worship of the old 'Sun God' to the Christian 'Son of God' was almost undetectable.

There is, however, absolutely no evidence biblical or otherwise for the birth of Christ actually being at this time of year and many historians and theological scholars actually favour the spring rather than the winter solstice.

To strengthen the case for the birth of Christ being celebrated around the solstice, however, other associated Christian festivals also began to spring up around this time in order to provide a firm Christian slant to the old Pagan celebrations.

The commemoration of the baptism of Christ by John the Baptist began to be celebrated on 6th January but was eventually superceded in importance by Matthew's account of the visit of the Magi to the Holy child, later known as the Epiphany.

All of these 'new' festivals, albeit with a few breaks, extended the Christmas period until 6th January. Indeed the Council of Tours in 567 CE stated that the period between the Nativity and Epiphany should become one occasion, but that the original three day Roman festival of the Kalendae between 1st and 3rd of January should be acknowledged as a fasting period between the festivities, due to the fact that there was no Christian connotation. This was accepted for a while, but by the eighth century the old New Year festival of Kalendae had regained its popularity.

Eventually, the church accepted that a three day fast was becoming increasingly difficult to impose and decided to Christianise the Kalendae festival by overlaying it with a Christian one, namely the 'Feast of Christ's Circumcision' on 1st January, thereby making the old Roman festival acceptable within the Christian regime.

Hence from the eighth century until the Middle Ages, the festival of Christmas and its twelve associated days became a firmly established tradition with feasting, games and church services becoming a familiar pattern throughout.

The now famous song entitled 'The Twelve Days of Christmas' was first printed in 1864 and, although not immediately obvious, is said to be rife with Christian symbolism.

On the first day of Christmas my true love sent to me a partridge in a pear tree.
(Jesus Christ)
On the second day of Christmas my true love sent to me two turtle doves.
(The Old and New Testaments)
On the third day of Christmas my true love sent to me three French hens.
(Christian virtues of faith, hope and charity)
On the fourth day of Christmas my true love sent to me four calling birds.
(The four Gospels)
On the fifth day of Christmas my true love sent to me five gold rings.
(The Pentateuch, first five books of the Old Testament)
On the sixth day of Christmas my true love sent to me six geese a-laying.
(The six days it to took God to create the universe)
On the seventh day of Christmas my true love sent to me seven swans a-swimming.
(The seven gifts of the Holy Spirit)
On the eighth day of Christmas my true love sent to me eight maids a-milking.
(The eight Beatitudes)
On the ninth day of Christmas my true love sent to me nine ladies dancing
(Nine fruits of the Holy Spirit)
On the tenth day of Christmas my true love sent to me ten lords a-leaping
(The Ten Commandments)
On the eleventh day of Christmas my true love sent to me eleven pipers piping
(The eleven faithful apostles)
On the twelfth day of Christmas my true love sent to me twelve

MRS DARLEY'S PAGAN WHISPERS

drummers drumming.
(The twelve points of doctrine in the Apostle's Creed)

Modern myth, however, tells us that the song came about much earlier than this, when Catholicism was illegal in Britain and Catholics felt compelled to 'go underground' and communicate their faith in the hidden symbolism of this particular carol.

Norse and Anglo Saxon influences

A more modern word, which has become synonymous with this time of year, is that of 'Yule', popularised during the Danish rule of Britain in the eleventh century and was thought to simply be the Anglicised version of the Danish term for Christmas, 'Juul'.

Although the origins of the word are somewhat uncertain, the Venerable Bede suggested its roots perhaps lay in the Anglo Saxon word 'hweal', meaning 'wheel', whilst other sources state that it comes from the Anglo Saxon word used to describe this festival, 'geola', which was pronounced 'Yula' and meant 'yoke' or 'circle'. Appropriate no doubt, in recognising the continuing circle or wheel of the year.

The festival of 'Twelfth Night', celebrated at the end of the festive period in January, was also influenced by Nordic and Saxon cultures and also became known as 'Wassail Night'.

The occasion of 'Wassailing' was first described in the 1320s by a writer who witnessed the host of a party holding a drinking bowl and shouting as a toast the word 'Wassail' before taking a drink of what was probably 'Lambswool', a mixture of mulled ale, herbs and honey. The word itself is thought to be a derivative of the Norse 'Wes Hail', or the Anglo Saxon 'Waes Hael', simply meaning 'good health' or 'Be whole', a term which was popular as far back as the eighth century.

After taking a drink, the cup was passed from person to person and accepted each time with a kiss. During the following century small cakes were dipped into the bowl and, during the Middle Ages, Wassailing became a very important part of the festival of

Twelfth Night, with silver cups often being used for the occasion. Songs soon accompanied the Wassail Bowl, one of which goes:

'Wassail, wassail all over the town
The toast it is white and the ale it is brown.'

In the apple growing areas of south western Britain, Wassailing also took on another dimension, and the custom of wishing 'Good health' to all who drank from the Wassail bowl extended to dancing out into the fields and orchards and bestowing good health on both the cattle and fruit trees, a custom which is thought to date back to Pagan times. In the eighteenth century, the *Gentleman's Magazine* reported an incident of how farm workers would circle what was considered to be the best apple tree in the orchard three times and sing:

'Here's to thee, old apple tree,
Whence thou mayst bud, and whence thou mayst blow,
Whence thou mayst bear apples enow!
Hats full! Caps full!
Three score bushels full!
And my pockets full too!
Huzza! Huzza! Huzza!

Wassailing customs varied throughout the country and included rapping the trunks with sticks or firing guns through the orchard to 'wake up' the trees, and pouring cider on the roots to encourage a good crop of apples. Some of these traditions are still carried out today in Somerset and Devon, although occasionally the date preferred is 17th January, which would have been old Twelfth Night, before the changes of the Gregorian calendar.

Other Cultures

For thousands of years, however, various ancient cultures have celebrated the return of the sun, or the birth of a son at this darkest time of year. The Persian sun God Mithras was born at the winter solstice, as was Osiris, God of the Egyptian underworld, Dionysus was the Greek God of wine and Shiva, the Indian Deity.

Breaks in continuity

It must be said, however, that simply because the twelve days of Christmas were more or less set in the medieval period, the festive period was not without its problems.

In Scotland the Christmas celebrations were abolished in 1561 when the newly reformed Scottish 'Kirk' split from the mainstream European thinking and claimed that the Catholic church had invented the feasts of Christmas, Circumcision and Epiphany, along with those of the Virgin Mary, the disciples and associated Saints. Indeed, those who continued to observe the Yuletide festivities were severely punished through the courts.

With the coming of the Civil War and puritan rule, however, Christmas was abolished throughout the rest of Britain between 1645 and 1660 and it was not until the return of Charles II to the throne that Christmas celebrations were once again allowed both in England and Scotland, although it took until 1665 for Elgin Cathedral to finally hold a Christmas service.

The power of the Scottish 'Kirk', however, remained persistently strong in the mid lowlands, and even as late as 1690 people were still punished for keeping the Christian festivals.

The need for a midwinter feast, however, still remained strong in the hearts of the Scots. Eventually a compromise was made and the winter festivities were transferred to New Year's Eve, which held little religious meaning compared to Christmas day itself.

The Scottish New Year Festival, known as 'Hogmanay', is thought to derive from a medieval French word 'Aguillanneuf', which was descriptive of a New Year's gift and today is still held dear within the Scottish heart.

Sacred Yuletide plants

The ancient Celts recognised just two seasons: winter, which began at Samhain on 31st October, and summer, which began at Beltane on 30th April at sunset. These two seasons came to be personified by the Oak King and the Holly King.

At the winter solstice, when the sun gradually won its battle to begin its long sojourn back to full strength, the Holly King (who ruled from the summer solstice) battled with the Oak King and the Oak King triumphed. It was he who wore the crown until the summer solstice, when the scenario was reversed.

To represent the two kings, we bring holly into the home to represent the Holly King and mistletoe to represent the Oak King, as mistletoe grows on Oak trees (although often found on apple trees). These two popular pieces of Yuletide greenery each have their own folklore and magical properties attached to them.

Holly

Holly has always been seen as a magical plant, due to its brightness and sharpness during the darkest time of year, and its very name is a derivation of the word 'holy'. Throughout the Celtic lands of Europe, holly was and still is said to protect against malevolent forces, poison and lightening. The latter was because it was a sacred tree to the Norse God Thor, who was the God of thunder and lightening, and many Norsemen would plant a holly tree near to their homes to protect them from lightening strikes.

The Holly King himself was often depicted in the Mummers plays, as a warlike giant who wielded a great wooden club made of a holly branch. He even weaved his way into Arthurian legends as the Green Knight, who challenged Sir Gawain to a duel during a Yuletide feast, holding only his branch of holly as a weapon.

Holly is often seen as the masculine principal in Yuletide greenery due to its prickly nature and the fact that the red berries depict the blood of the God as he lays down his life for the sake of the earth's fertility. However, in sharp contrast to this view, holly has also been regarded purely as a feminine symbol due to the red berries being the associated colour of menstruation.

Perhaps, therefore, holly is androgynous, in that it can pay homage to both the God and Goddess. An old Saxon tradition states that if the household wreath is made of 'he' holly (holly without berries) then the husband will rule the house for the coming year, but if the wreath is made from 'she' holly (holly with berries) then it is the wife who will rule the household for the coming year!

Holly legends have also made their way into Christianity, via the Roman church. Holly was once said to be a deciduous tree, until Herod's soldiers came to slay Jesus. At Mary's request, the holly tree regained its leaves in winter so that she could hide her child in the foliage. Another Christian legend states that the holly berries were once white, until touched by the blood of Christ as part of the crown of thorns.

Mistletoe

Although mistletoe is very much the magical feminine partner to holly's masculine principal, it also has occasionally been regarded as the masculine to holly's feminine, due to its white berries being regarded as the representation of semen against the red menstrual berries of holly.

Whilst mistletoe, like holly, confers protection and, allegedly, invisibility if worn around the neck, it does have more sinister connotations. The Celtic Druids were well versed in the use of mistletoe to strengthen their magical workings, to encourage lucid dreams and its use as a mind-altering drug when it came to human sacrifice.

When Lindow man was discovered in a peat bog just outside Manchester, forensic evidence showed that he had been the victim of a ritualistic threefold killing.

In the first instance he received a number of heavy blows to the head, which would have rendered him unconscious. Secondly his neck was broken with a cord, which would have caused physical death. Finally his throat was cut, and the future divined from his flowing blood.

Naturally this sounds quite horrific and barbaric to us now. However, the Celts did show some compassion towards their unfortunate victim. When his stomach contents were investigated, it was found that he had been given a concoction of mistletoe, which would have provided him with an altered state of consciousness before the horrific ritual began.

Legend has it that the Druids would cut mistletoe from the oak tree with a golden sickle on the sixth night of the new moon and hand it out to the community at religious ceremonies, where it was known as 'all heal'. They would also place it on their altars at the winter solstice as an offering to the Gods.

A legend concerning the origins of kissing under the mistletoe wends its way to us from Scandinavian mythology, where Baldur, the much loved God of peace, was slain by Loki, God of destruction, by an arrow made from mistletoe. Outraged by Baldur's death, the other Deities demanded that his life be restored. Eventually this request was complied with and, as a token of thanks, Baldur's mother, the Goddess Frigga, hung up a piece of mistletoe and promised to kiss all those who passed beneath it!

Mistletoe, however, has never really made its way into Christian legend, as during the early Christian period it was seen very much as both a heathen plant and a powerful symbol of fertility and as such was forbidden inside any church, although this does seem to have changed from the seventeenth century onwards according to church records.

There is a particular instance, which is recorded in Brand's book *Popular Antiquities*, where an old Sexton of Teddington Church once told him that mistletoe was taken into the church by mistake and, upon seeing it, the vicar instantly ordered its removal!

In medieval times, however, York Minster gave full honour to mistletoe on Christmas Eve, where it was carried to the high altar after which a universal pardon and liberty for all was proclaimed at the four gates of the city for as long as the mistletoe remained on the altar!

This rather 'out of place' church custom may have been due to the fact that, for a hundred years, York remained the capital of the Scandinavian Kingdom founded by Halfdan in 875 AD and as we have seen mistletoe played a significant part in Norse myth and legend.

Ivy

This is seen as the true feminine partner to holly and is protective in nature. It is said that if ivy grows on the walls of a house then the occupants will be protected from misfortune.

In more recent times it was often said that to bring more ivy into the house at Christmas than holly would bring bad luck. However, this could have been a mere patriarchal fear of female supremacy. Perhaps balance is what we should all strive towards?

The Fir Tree

The Christmas tree was introduced into Britain by Prince Albert in 1841. However, the tradition of having a Christmas tree was known in parts of Northern Europe as early as the mid sixteenth century. It is thought that the custom actually originated in Roman times during the Saturnalia celebrations where trees were liberally decorated.

Solstice colours

Colours associated with this time of year include red, green and gold. Red represents the blood of life, and the sacrificial nature of the male principal. Green represents the vegetation that surrounds and sustains us, as well as the eternal presence of the Goddess, whilst gold represents the sun gaining in strength as it journeys once again toward the summer solstice.

Carole Carlton

The Yule Log

It is difficult to date the origins of this tradition as the first written accounts do not appear until the seventeenth century, however many references state that it is most certainly Pagan and possibly of Norse origin.

The Yule log, whether of oak or ash, played an important part in the winter solstice celebrations and everyone who took part in the ritual was said to have good fortune. Lighting the Yule log was a form of sympathetic magic, which was believed to encourage the sun to shine more brightly as it grew in strength. A piece of the Yule log was always kept in order that the following year's fire could be lit from it, whilst the ashes were often spread on the fields to ensure a good harvest.

In today's modern world of very few 'real' fires, the original Yule log is now replaced by a chocolate one, although the tradition of keeping a little bit until next year should perhaps be given a miss!

Who is Father Christmas or Santa Claus?

Santa Claus, or Father Christmas, have today become interchangeable names for the lovable fantasy figure who materialises with presents on Christmas Eve complete with reindeer and sleigh. Initially, however, they were very separate figures.

Professor Ronald Hutton tells us that the character actually developed over a 250-year period following a play by Ben Jonson in 1616 where the presenter was a rather humorous figure dressed in a hat, hose, scarf and beard. This character gradually became known as 'Lord Christmas' or more popularly as 'Father Christmas'. He was not, however, anything to do with children, but merely a presenter of adult games and feasting.

To become familiar with the origins of Santa Claus we must look to St Nicholas, the Bishop of Myra in Turkey, during the fourth century AD. He was the patron Saint of fishermen, bankers, bakers and particularly children, whose feast day was celebrated on 6th December

In one legend we are told that he miraculously restored three schoolboys back to life after being murdered by an innkeeper, who then placed their dismembered bodies in a pickling jar!

On this Saint's day parents would place presents in their children's shoes (later to become stockings) and say they were from the Saint in return for the children being good during the year. This Turkish custom was carried across Europe and from there taken by Dutch and German settlers to America where, after initial success, the custom gradually waned.

In 1822, a New York Professor wrote a poem to his children, entitled *A visit from St Nicholas*. This was subsequently sent to a local newspaper and became an overnight success, having been accompanied by an illustration which depicted him being dressed in fur, sporting a big white beard and being driven across the sky by reindeer.

The figure of St Nicholas was therefore gradually transformed into the more popular figure of Santa Claus that we know today, and his custom of present giving was moved to coincide with Christmas Eve.

Customs associated with St Nicholas, however, are attributed to more ancient roots. One source states that Woden (equivalent to the Norse God Odin), the ancient God of the Europeans and subsequently the Britons, was the original St Nicholas. He was often depicted as riding through the sky and taking gifts during the hours of darkness to those who honoured him.

Woden is also depicted as Cernunnos, the Celtic Horned God, whom we meet at the spring equinox. The Horned God is normally depicted as stag-like in appearance with magnificent antlers. The antlers of the horned God have therefore been handed over to the reindeer, whilst the present-giving attributes of Woden have been maintained, but all under the acceptable Christian guise of St Nicholas, or Santa Claus.

Interestingly the original Santa Claus outfit was green, which would have been in keeping with Cernunnos' as the 'green man'.

However, his suit was changed to red during an advertising campaign by Coca Cola during the 1930s, to make him the jolly red clad figure we all know and love today.

Modern additions to the festive period

Boxing Day

Originally known as the Christian 'Feast of St Stephen' (a name which is still retained in Southern Ireland), the term 'Boxing Day' became part and parcel of the English language during the Victorian era, although it was actually named after a custom made popular during the seventeenth century.

Here apprentices of all kinds would keep an earthenware box into which monetary gifts were dropped and, upon becoming full, the box would be broken open and the apprentice would be able to treat himself for the festive period. Eventually this extended to servants and then trades people to enable them to have a little extra money over the Christmas period.

Traditional Fayre

During the fifteenth and sixteenth centuries the wealthy often ate boar's head, which was trumpeted to the table. It was a revered meat and once highly prized by the ancient Celts and Norsemen. At Hornchurch as late as the early twentieth century a boar's head was provided every year from tithe money, garlanded with bay leaves and carried by a procession of people on Christmas Day afternoon to a field adjacent to the church where it was wrestled for by the people of the village.

Eventually the boar and other exotic meats such as swan and peacock were superceded by roast beef and this in turn was replaced by the cheaper turkey during Victorian times, although there are records of turkey being served as early as 1542.

One account of Christmas fayre as shown in the Newcastle Chronicle of 6th January 1770 describes a Christmas pie made for a certain Sir Henry Grey and contained the following: *'4 Geese, 2 Turkeys, 4 Wild Ducks, 2 Rabbits, 2 Curlews, 7 Blackbirds, 6 Pigeons, 4 Partridges, 6 Snipe, 2 Woodcock, 2 Neats' Tongues. The pastry was made from 2 bushels of flour and 20 LB's of Butter!'*

Plum porridge became thicker and thicker until it eventually gave way to our more familiar Christmas pudding, which first appeared around 1670. It also became the hiding place for silver coins considered to be symbols of good luck, which originally were placed in the more traditional twelfth night cake.

Christmas Carols

The word 'Carol' refers to a form of verse rather than a particular type of song, and it is thought that the roots of this verse form lie within the monasteries of the early Christian church. Carols, however, were also synonymous with a particular form of dance and the two went hand in hand until the fifteenth century, when the dance was abandoned but the song or verse form survived. Some of these songs had Christian themes attached to them and these began to be known as 'Christmas Carols', whilst the remainder continued to be called simply 'Carols'. There is, however, little evidence to show that they were sung in church and they were more likely to be sung around the fire at home, or from door to door, as is still the custom today.

A Winter Solstice Tale

The cottage reminded me of a woodland grotto. Every beam, shelf and lintel carried an array of winter foliage, from fir and mistletoe to holly and ivy, all interwoven with cones, cinnamon sticks and red ribbon. The aroma of the greenery, combined with sweet wood smoke from the fire and mulled wine from the kitchen, made a heady concoction and was truly a feast for the senses.

'Here we are dear,' said Mrs Darley. 'Happy Solstice!' A cup of mulled wine made its way into my hands as I sat curled up in the big armchair beside the fire. The wine was closely followed by edible seasonal goodies to which I easily fell victim.

Never being one to be idle for long, Mrs Darley placed her mulled wine on the table and walked over to a huge wooden chest, which sat in the corner of the room and about which I had always been intrigued. She turned the key and slowly opened the lid. Curios, I moved to the edge of my seat and watched her take out a small wooden box, which she placed on the table.

'Come dear,' she said, 'let's have some fun and I will tell you a little about yourself.' She patted the seat beside her at the table and reluctantly I moved from the warm fireside.

As I sat down, Mrs Darley opened the lid of the small wooden box and I suddenly became aware of the most exquisite aromas.

'What are they?' I asked, looking down at a collection of tiny brown bottles.

'Essential oils dear, a precious gift from Mother Earth.'

We then began a strange game, where I was given six oils to smell and was asked to state my favourite. I knew that as soon as I had smelled the fifth oil no other could compare to it. It was almost ethereal, with a haunting addictive quality.

'Ah yes, I should have known,' she smiled. 'This oil is normally chosen by someone who is opening up to their own truth, a seeker on the spiritual path.'

'What is it?' I asked.

'Frankincense,' she said, 'most apt for this time of year! This is a time to be still in your centre before dancing outward and radiating your light to the world. As the sun begins its journey, so you must begin yours.'

She raised her cup of mulled wine.

'To your journey,' she said.

'To my journey,' I whispered.

Celebrating Yuletide

This is a time of joyful preparation and celebration in welcoming

MRS DARLEY'S PAGAN WHISPERS

the rebirth of the sun, and Mrs Darley's cottage was always a hive of activity as the winter solstice approached.

Candles were always the first item we made as December dawned, albeit we cheated a little as Mrs Darley would order sheets of beeswax from the bee farm on the north coast in the festive colours of red, green and gold. These would be cut into right-angled triangles, a piece of wick cut to size and drizzled with an essential oil of the season such as frankincense, myrrh, cinnamon or orange and then rolled tightly to make an attractive centre piece for the table or mantelpiece.

Making solstice crackers always ensured a fun filled evening, although the contents varied slightly from the Christmas crackers with which we were all familiar. Mrs Darley's crackers were made from gold, red or green card and had to contain a sweet, a small gift of our choice and a few words of wisdom appropriate to the season. They were then placed into a hessian sack and over a seasonal drink we would all draw a cracker and derive great pleasure from our gift and the words of wisdom. Sadly, however, they remained silent when pulled!

Swags made from seasonal greenery always rounded off our festive craft sessions in readiness to welcome the return of the sun.

Inner Reflections at Yule

This is a time of giving thanks and celebrating all that our life contains. This does not mean simply material possessions, but important things like love, relationships, creative skills and health, as well as food and shelter, very much the things our ancestors would have appreciated. It is appropriate therefore that we all enjoy this lovely season, share each other's company, play games, exchange small gifts and share festive food together.

It is an occasion upon which to be generous, not perhaps with money and expensive gifts, but with our time and our thoughts. Use it as an opportunity to contact people who have become distanced from us for whatever reason during the year or to perhaps give time to those who really need it, including ourselves! Life is fleeting and often spent harbouring past hurts instead of moving on to a more rewarding future.

Give a small gift to someone who would not normally feature on your seasonal list, or perhaps donate something to a charity or other deserving cause, whether this is by way of a present, money or your time. You may wish to invite someone into your home who you know will be spending their time alone. In this way you can bring the light into someone else's life and in return it will shine in yours.

The Goddess at this time shows us her triple faced aspect, encouraging us to revel and celebrate all aspects of our true selves.

First and foremost the Goddess in her mother aspect gives birth her son and this is, therefore, an ideal time for us to contemplate and incubate new ideas, even though they may not yet be fully formed enough to make their mark on the world.

She also shows us the face of the wise Crone as she waits in the darkness and prepares for her transformation at the next festival of Imbolc. The Crone encourages us to treasure the wisdom we have gained throughout the year and to use it well as we journey forward into the light on the wings of the maiden who will, once again, call the young at heart to taste the freedom of an awaiting spring.

Winter Solstice Dedication

Find somewhere you will not be disturbed, burn essential oils or incense of your choice and play music of you wish. Take into the room a drink (alcoholic or otherwise), something light to eat, a lighter or matches and one or more candles, either of gold, red or green to represent the return of the sun, the blood of life and the continuing presence of the Goddess (white will always suffice if you do not have coloured candles).

When you feel ready, dim the lights and light your candle(s).

Now still your mind for a moment or two and become aware of

the aroma you have chosen to burn. When you are ready you may use the dedication below to address the God and the Goddess, or of course you may wish to write your own. Enjoy this quiet time for as long as you wish and when you have finished, raise a glass to toast the occasion and have something to eat to ground yourself. When you blow out the candles, ask that the energy from the flame be sent somewhere it is needed, rather than direct its path yourself.

The Triple Goddess and Infant Lord

To the wisdom of the Crone in the darkness,
To the innocence of the Maiden who awaits,
To the love of the Mother in her labour,
To the birth of the Child who will be Lord.
Lord, we welcome you.
Lady, we honour you.

Fate

Out of the shadows
Out of the gloom,
Klotho spins, man forth
From the womb.

The Moirai gather,
They weave and plan,
The Moirai fashion
The fate of man.

Out of the shadows
Out of the gloom,
Lachesis weaves, man's
Life on her loom.

The Moirai gather

Carole Carlton

They weave and plan,
The Moirai fashion
The fate of man.

Out of the shadows
Out of the gloom,
Atropos calls, man
Back to the tomb.

The Moirai gather
They weave and plan,
The Moirai fashion
The fate of man.

Chapter 11

A Promise of Tomorrow

This is not the end, but merely the beginning of a journey, which hopefully will be made over and over again. Each time the wheel spins a new adventure begins. Each spring will be lovelier, each summer will be filled with new pleasures, each autumn will look richer and more vibrant than the last and each winter will bring more opportunities to rest and reflect.

This is a journey, which can enrich our lives and teach us to sit up and appreciate what happens outside our window. It invites us to make footprints in the snow, run barefoot in the grass and swish the swirling leaves beneath our feet. It invites us to be a part of nature and the living earth, just as our ancestors have been for millennia.

Take time to consider this sojourn around the wheel and spare a moment to reflect, rejoice, or even shed a tear for the experiences the year has brought. Nothing ever happens without reason, welcome both the joys and the sorrows, for each enables us to gain in strength and grow through our experiences. Every life event shapes who and what we are, so that we may in turn enrich, enlighten and help the lives of others we may meet along the path.

Life is a journey, an adventure, a continually moving experience through which we should ebb and flow. Just as the sun waxes and wanes, just as the triple faced Goddess turns from Maiden to Mother and from Mother to Crone, so we should savour every changing moment as own our life cycle turns from spring to summer, and from autumn into winter.

The gift of our ancestors was one of wisdom and insight. Listen to the whispers of yesterday and rejoice in the promise of a brighter tomorrow.

Some Other Titles From Mirage Publishing

A Prescription from The Love Doctor: How to find Love in 7 Easy Steps - Dr Joanne 'The Love Doctor' Coyle
Burnt: One Man's Inspiring Story of Survival - Ian Colquhoun
Cosmic Ordering Guide - Stephen Richards
Cosmic Ordering Connection - Stephen Richards
Cosmic Ordering: Chakra Clearing - Stephen Richards
Cosmic Ordering: Oracle Healing Cards – Stephen Richards
Cosmic Ordering: Oracle Wish Cards – Stephen Richards & Karen Whitelaw Smith
Past Life Tourism - Barbara Ford-Hammond
The Butterfly Experience: Inspiration For Change - Karen Whitelaw Smith
The Real Office: An Uncharacteristic Gesture of Magnanimity by Management Supremo Hilary Wilson-Savage - Hilary Wilson-Savage
The Tumbler: Kassa (Košice) – Auschwitz – Sweden - Israel - Azriel Feuerstein

Fothcoming titles
Life Without Lottie - Fiona Fridd
Psychic Salon - Barbara Ford-Hammond
Rebel Diet™: They Don't Want You To Have It! – Emma James

Mirage Publishing Website:
www.miragepublishing.com

Submissions of Mind, Body & Spirit manuscripts welcomed from new authors.